Hilton Head Island Travel Guide, South Carolina, USA

Gullah History and Tradition,

Author
David Mills.

Publisher:
SONITTEC LTD
College House, 2nd Floor
17 King Edwards Road,
Ruislip
London
HA4 7AE.

Table of Content

Summary

The world is a book and those who do not travel read only one page.

It is indeed very unfortunate that some people feel traveling is a sheer waste of time, energy and money. Some also find traveling an extremely boring activity. Nevertheless, a good majority of people across the world prefer traveling, rather than staying inside the confined spaces of their homes. They love to explore new places, meet new people, and see things that they would not find in their homelands. It is this very popular attitude that has made tourism, one of the most profitable, commercial sectors in the world.

People travel for various reasons. Some travel for work, others for fun, and some for finding mental peace. Though every person may have his/her own reason to go on a journey, it is essential to note that traveling, in itself, has some inherent advantages. For one, for some days getting away from everyday routine is a pleasant change. It not only refreshes one's body, but also mind and soul. Traveling to a distant place and doing exciting things that are not thought of otherwise, can rejuvenate a person, who then returns home, ready to take on new and more difficult challenges in life and work. It makes a person forget his worries, problems, frustrations, and fears, albeit for some time. It gives him a chance to think wisely and constructively. Traveling also helps to heal; it can mend a broken heart.

For many people, traveling is a way to attain knowledge, and perhaps, a quest to find answers to their questions. For this, many people prefer to go to faraway and isolated places. For believers, it is a search for God and to gain higher knowledge; for others, it is a search for inner peace. They might or might not find what they are looking for, but such an experience certainly enriches their lives

Introduction

Hilton Head Island is a semi-tropical barrier island located on the Intracostal Waterway off of the South Carolina Atlantic Coast, about 90 miles south of Charlestonand 40 north of Savannah. It is world-renowned for its pristine beaches, abundant golf courses, superb tennis facilities and picturesque natural environment of seascapes, salt marshes, lagoons, tall pine forests, magnolias and majestic moss-draped oaks, Hilton Head attracts approximately 2.5 million annual visitors.

At 12 miles long and 5 miles wide, Hilton Head Island is the largest barrier island between Long Island and the Bahamas. Development at this popular travel destination has been comparatively restrained by stringent standards set forth in 1956 by visionary Charles Fraser's master plan for the island's first resort community, Sea Pines Plantation. The Sea Pines Plantation plan established Hilton Head Island as the first Eco-planned resort destination in the United States. Today, Hilton Head Island contains several environmentally planned residential and resort communities. Neon signs, bright street lights, and tall buildings are not permitted, allowing visitors and residents to *see the stars at night.*

A good first stop for your visit is the Hilton Head Island Welcome Center, where you can collect maps, brochures on local activities, schedules of upcoming events and more. Also, check for discounts on attractions, golf, dining, fishing, accommodations.

History

Incorporated as a town in 1983, Hilton Head Island is home to more than 40,000 residents who live year-round in our renowned environmentally planned resort and residential communities. Yet much of the Island remains as it was when sighted from William Hilton's ship more than 350 years ago. Over the centuries, Hilton Head Island's natural beauty, spectacular seascapes, exceptional ecology and South Carolina historical sites have beckoned generations of explorers—with Native Americans, English, Spanish, French colonists, pirates, African-Americans and soldiers all leaving their footprints on the sands of South Carolina's

Treasured Coast. And now is the time for you to leave your own footprints in the sand…on Hilton Head Island.

Earliest Inhabitants

When William Hilton landed in the Lowcountry in 1663, he was greeted by Spanish-speaking Indians from the Yemassee tribe, who had migrated north from Florida 100 years prior. He also encountered the native Escamacus Indians, but little is known of the earlier native civilization that inhabited the Island as far back as 4,000 years ago. Remnants of mysterious shell rings, measuring up to 240 feet across and nine feet high, can still be found on the Island. Yet, like the enigmatic rocks of Stonehenge and the carvings of Easter Island, their secrets remain hidden. Today, you can view these artifacts of Hilton Head Island history at Sea Pines Forest

Preserve and on the north end of the Island, off Squire Pope Road in Green Shell Park.

Plantation Life

In 1698, the Lord Proprietors granted several islands and some of the Lowcountry's mainland to John Bayley. While the entire area was named Bayley's Barony, Hilton Head Island was referred to as Trench's Island, in honor of Alexander Trench, the Bayley's property agent and collector of land-lease fees.

John Barnwell became Hilton Head Island's first English settler in 1717 after receiving a grant of 1,000 acres in what is now Hilton Head Plantation. However, Hilton Head Island did not gain worldwide recognition until 1790 when another planter, William Elliott, successfully raised the first crop of long-staple Sea Island cotton. Elliott, with the help of his neighbor, Will Seabrook, pioneered a new type of fertilizer for the cotton, resulting in record crops and wide acclaim for the Sea Island cotton.

By 1860, 24 plantations were in operation on Hilton Head Island. Although the main crop was cotton, indigo, sugar cane, rice, and other crops also were cultivated. Due to the land's low elevation and hot summers, the wealthy landowners spent little time on the Island, opting to locate their beautiful townhouses in less tropical environments on the mainland.

Zion Chapel of Ease Cemetery and Baynard Mausoleum

The antebellum Zion Chapel of Ease Cemetery and Baynard Mausoleum, situated among ancient moss draped oaks and facing the waters of Broad Creek, is the burial place of several of Hilton Head Island's original colonial families. The chapel was completed in 1788 and the Baynard Mausoleum was built in 1846. It is the oldest structure still standing on the island, and more Revolutionary War soldiers are buried in this coastal cemetery than anywhere else on the coast other than Charleston. Named to the National Register of Historic Places, the cemetery and mausoleum is owned and maintained by the Heritage Library and the site is open to the public for respectful visits.

Civil War

Eleven months after South Carolina seceded from the Union, the shots fired on Fort Sumter reverberated on Hilton Head Island. On November 7, 1861, the Island became the scene of the largest amphibious landing by U.S forces until D-Day, as more than 12,000 Union soldiers landed on the Island. In less than five hours, the Union fleet captured both Fort Beauregard on St. Philips Island

and Fort Walker on Hilton Head Island. The Island fell into the hands of Federal troops, forcing Island families to evacuate their plantation homes.

The Civil War and the subsequent abolition of slavery altered the prosperous and patrician lifestyle of the plantation owners forever. After assuming command in September of 1862, General Ormsby Mitchel was upset at the living conditions of the former slaves. He confiscated some land on Confederate General Thomas Fenwick Drayton's Fish Haul Plantation, laid put streets and lots, and provided lumber for the former slaves to build their homes in a town that would be called Mitchelville. It was the first self-governing town of formerly enslaved African Americans. After the war, as the freed slaves on the island attempted to grow Sea Island cotton, the boll weevil proved to be even more devastating. Consequently, Hilton

Head Island lapsed into obscurity, remaining isolated for over 80 years.

During this period, the Island maintained a small population of mostly the descendants of former slaves. They survived modestly on small farms and as hunters and fisherman. Their Gullah culture and language survive today as a living legacy of their strength and perseverance.

In the late 1940's, the Island experienced a sort of re-birth when a group of timbermen recognized great potential in the Island's tall, straight pines. Popularly called sea pines, the trees produced lumber for a variety of uses.

The First Resort

In 1956, Charles Fraser, son of one of the families that owned most of the Island, realized that Hilton Head Island had more to offer than just timber.

Armed with vision, energy, modern air conditioning and investment dollars, he created a master plan for a resort community. His efforts were aided by the construction of a bridge to the mainland the same year. The first of the Hilton Head family resorts—Sea Pines Plantation— became the prototype of the modern resort community, now copied around the world.

Incorporated as a town in 1983, Hilton Head Island is now home to several environmentally planned resort and residential communities, supporting more than 40,000 full-time residents. These communities have been named "plantations" but cotton fields have been replaced by lush green golf courses, tennis courts, shimmering lakes and beautifully designed resorts and villas.

Despite this development, much of the Island remains as it was when sighted from William

Hilton's ship more than 300 years ago. Hilton Head Island's natural beauty, spectacular seascapes, exceptional ecology and South Carolina historical sites now beckon a new generation of explorers.

Gullah History

The Gullah are African Americans who live in the Lowcountry region of South Carolina and Georgia, which includes both the coastal plain and the Beaufort Sea Islands.

The Gullah are known for preserving more of their African linguistic and cultural heritage than any other African-American community in the United States. They speak an English-based creole language containing many African loanwords and significant influences from African languages in grammar and sentence structure; Gullah storytelling, cuisine, music, folk beliefs, crafts, farming and fishing traditions, all exhibit strong influences from West and Central African cultures.

Most of the Gullahs' early ancestors in what is now the United States were brought to the South Carolina and Georgia Lowcountry through the ports of Charleston and Savannah as slaves. Charleston was one of the most important ports in North America for the Transatlantic slave trade. Up to half of the enslaved Africans brought into what is now the United States came through that port. A great majority of the remaining flowed through Savannah, which was also active in the slave trade.

The largest group of enslaved Africans brought into Charleston and Savannah came from the West African rice-growing region. South Carolina and Georgia rice planters once called this region the "Rice Coast", indicating its importance as a source of skilled African labor for the North American rice industry. Once it was discovered that rice would grow in the southern U.S. regions, it was assumed that enslaved Africans from rice-growing regions in Africa would be beneficial, due to their knowledge of rice-growing techniques. By the middle of the 18th century, the South Carolina and Georgia Lowcountry was covered by thousands of acres of rice fields. African farmers from the "Rice Coast" brought the skills for cultivation and tidal irrigation that made rice one of the most successful industries in early America.

The semi-tropical climate that made the Lowcountry such an excellent place for rice production also made it vulnerable to the spread of malaria and yellow fever. Fearing disease, many white planters left the Lowcountry during the rainy spring and summer months when fever ran rampant and they left their African "rice drivers," or overseers, in charge of the plantations. Working on large plantations with hundreds of laborers, and with African traditions reinforced by new imports from the same regions, the Gullahs developed a culture in which elements of African languages, cultures, and community life were preserved to a high degree. Their culture was quite different from that of slaves in states like Virginia and North Carolina, where slaves lived in smaller settlements and had more sustained and frequent interactions with whites.

Civil War Period

When the U.S. Civil War began, the Union rushed to blockade Confederate shipping. White planters on the Sea Islands, fearing an invasion by the US naval forces, abandoned their plantations and fled to the mainland. When Union forces arrived on the Sea Islands in 1861, they found the Gullah people eager for their freedom, and eager as well to defend it.

The Union quickly occupied Beaufort and many Gullahs served with distinction in the Union Army's First South Carolina Volunteers. Beaufort's Sea Islands were the first place in the South where slaves were freed. Long before the War ended, Quaker missionaries from Pennsylvania came down to start schools for the newly freed slaves. Penn Center, now a Gullah community organization on St. Helena Island, South Carolina, began as the very first school for freed slaves.

After the Civil War ended, the Gullahs' isolation from the outside world actually increased in some respects. The rice planters on the mainland gradually abandoned their farms and moved away from the area because of labor issues and hurricane damage to crops. Left alone in remote rural areas in the Lowcountry, the Gullahs continued to practice their traditional culture with little influence from the outside world well into the 20th Century. .

Celebrating & Protecting The Gullah Culture

In recent years the Gullah people—led by Penn Center and other determined community groups— have been persistent in keeping control of their traditional lands. In 2005, the Gullah community unveiled a translation of the New Testament in the Gullah language, a project that took more than 20 years to complete. The Gullahs achieved another victory in 2006 when the U.S. Congress passed the "Gullah/Geechee Cultural Heritage Corridor Act" that provides $10 million over ten years for the preservation and interpretation of historic sites relating to Gullah culture. The "heritage corridor" extends from southern North Carolina to northern Florida. The project will be administered by the US National Park Service with extensive consultation with the Gullah community.

Over the years, the Gullahs have attracted many historians, linguists, folklorists, and anthropologists interested in their rich cultural heritage. Many academic books on that subject have been published. The Gullah have also become a symbol of cultural pride for blacks throughout the United States and a subject of general interest in the media. This has given rise to countless newspaper and magazine articles, documentary films, and children's books on Gullah culture, and to a number of popular novels set in the Gullah region.

Gullah people now organize cultural festivals every year in towns up and down the Lowcountry. the Gullah Celebration on Hilton Head Island in February, The Gullah Festival in Beaufort in May, and Heritage Days at Penn Center on St. Helena Island in November.

[Have you ever heard the phrase, "Don't eat anything your grandmother wouldn't recognize"? The Gullah/Geechee of South Carolina most certainly understand its meaning, as they bring the recipes, culinary point of view and local ingredients of their ancestors into the 21st-century food scene.

In the 1700s, West Africans from countries like Sierra Leone, Guinea and Liberia were hand-picked and enslaved by plantation owners for their knowledge of rice cultivation in hot, humid climates like those of the Lowcountry and Sea Islands of South Carolina's coast. Many years later, after emancipation and the construction of bridges to and from the mainland, the customs of the Gullah people spread throughout the area and their spiritual, musical and culinary traditions eventually became part of South Carolina's cultural identity.

Now residents and visitors of the Palmetto State are embracing Gullah food culture more than ever, with restaurants from the mountains to the coast serving up Gullah classics like shrimp and grits, gumbo and Frogmore Stew. In fact, many of the dishes South Carolinians consider classic Southern favorites are actually derived from Gullah culture. Rice, for example - a Southern staple on its own or traditionally served with gumbo, gravy and stews - would've never survived in this area without the Gullah people's expert cultivation techniques.

The South's one-pot wonders are also thanks to Gullah culinary tradition. As the Gullah/Geechee worked on South Carolina plantations, they would stew whole vegetables in large pots and let them simmer all day long as they tended the fields. When they returned for supper, the vegetables would be tenderized and perfect for enjoying with homegrown rice and leftover meats from the master's table. The Gullah cooks are the originators of South Carolina's farm-to-table movement, and using the same local, seasonal ingredients and cooking techniques of their ancestors, the new generation of the Gullah/Geechee are propelling the time-honored dishes of their storied past into the mainstream.]

Gullah Cuisine

Like a good gumbo, Gullah cooking was and is still, layered with ingredients, flavors and cooking techniques borrowed over time from many cultures West African, European, Caribbean and even native American.

Likewise, many beloved "Southern" specialties can be directly accredited to the Gullah and their ancestral African cooking techniques. Peanuts, okra, rice, yams, peas, hot peppers, sesame seeds, sorghum, and watermelon are some of the foods brought across the sea to America by the Gullah's enslaved ancestors.

Does the aroma of hardwood-smoked, pit-cooked barbeque set your taste buds on alert? Does the thought of crispy, fried chicken or bowl of spicy shrimp okra gumbo fill your head with delight? Then say a word of 'thanks' to the Gullah as those and many more American favorites are of their making.

Combined with a love of family and a penchant for entertaining, to the Gullah, food is not merely for human sustenance, but a means for expressing love and appreciation for their families and community a very Southern notion, indeed.

Gullah Traditions

The sea islands of Charleston including property on Kiawah, Seabrook, and Johns Island are modernly known for prestigious beaches, tony topography, and private residences. However, as the good Gullah people frequently say, "Cumya can't tell binya," which simply means those who have come here (cumya) can't tell those who have been here (binya) how to live. The spirit, knowledge, and heritage of the coastal land largely belong to the Gullah natives, a group of African Americans who originated from West Africa and were enslaved and specifically brought to the South Carolina coast in the 1700s because of their knowledge of planting rice. As a colony, South Carolina benefited from the Gullah slaves' success with rice crops and, as a result, became one of wealthiest thirteen colonies. A close knit community, the Gullah, or "Geechie" people had more freedom than other groups of slaves simply because white plantation owners could not deal with the sweltering summer heat and maddening mosquitoes. Furthermore, owners relied on the Gullah people to teach them how to properly grow crops in a coastal environment. Ironically, the slaves were the masters of the craft and the masters were the students. After emancipation, many of the Gullah descendants opted to stay in the Lowcountry, thus gifting South Carolina with a rich cultural heritage.

Today, the Gullah tribe and traditions still actively permeate the real estate in Mt. Pleasant, Charleston, Kiawah, Seabrook, and Johns Island. From familiar spiritual songs to African-inspired dances to delicious home-made stews, the Gullah descendants proudly protect their heritage and invite residents and visitors alike to celebrate it with them. As an example, locals and tourists tarry off the trail to get their soul food fix at authentic Charleston Gullah restaurants such as Bertha's

Kitchen on Meeting Street, Hannibal's Kitchen on Blake Street (near Trident Tech Palmer Campus), and Martha Lou's Kitchen on Morrison Drive. No surprise, these restaurants along with other area Gullah restaurants are growing in popularity. The New York Times recently featured Martha Lou's restaurant in an article, which subsequently has generated more traffic in her restaurant. At 85 years young, Martha Lou is still the one in charge of the kitchen and serves classic Gullah dishes such as okra stew, chittlings, and bread pudding (Giddick 2015).

Apart from soul food and songs, many folks long for a Charleston sweetgrass basket, which are hand-made by Gullah/Geechie descendants. Like folklore, the art of basket-weaving is passed down from generation to generation and is a revered skill. The baskets are sturdy enough to hold work boots and crops but majestic enough to display as décor in many lowcountry homes. Though historically the Gullah men made the baskets out of bulrush for use on the plantation or for extra income, after emancipation, the women began to carefully create smaller sweetgrass baskets to hold fruits and vegetables. Today, Mt. Pleasant is the mecca of Charleston sweetgrass basketry, with several stands alongside Highway 17 North. Basket booths are also found at the market in downtown Charleston and along scenic Highway 61 towards Kiawah and Seabrook islands. The family of the late Mary Vanderhorst, a well-known sweetgrass basket artisan in Mt. Pleasant, offers a wide variety of baskets available for purchase online at www.charlestonbaskets.com. Prices range from $40 for a drink coaster to more than $6,000 for a custom piece. The baskets are not only functional but also excrete a subtle, sweet scent, which naturally freshens the indoor air.

From economic notoriety because of the rice crops to the introduction of soul food stews to the glorious art of basketry, Charleston is not Charleston without the contributions of the Gullah/Geechie nation. So whether buying real estate on Kiawah or Seabrook Islands or just visiting the historical sites around the Lowcountry, take time to salute the "binyas"; for their traditions transcend modern time.

Gullah Language

"All duh people wut come from africa aw oberseas wuz call Golla and dey talk wut call Golla talk." - Georgia,1936

Until quite recently, it was commonly believed that those who spoke Gullah were speaking what many termed broken English.Â" Few realized that this language is living evidence of a remarkable transformation that took place from Africa to

African American culture. People speaking Gullah is a testimony to one of the great acts of human endurance in the history of the world, the survival of African people away from home.

In the early times, slave holders and their visitors on the rice plantations often commented on the presence of the distinct language among the slave population. They had no idea that they were witnesses to a cultural phenomenon. Right before their eyes were the transformation, adaptation and persistence of a culture.

During the times, our people came from different language and culture groups, and geographical regions. They were brought here to be the main labor force in the rice and cotton industries, responsible for the planting, hoeing, ditching, pounding, plowing, basket making, winnowing, picking, and threshing. It goes without saying that communication was necessary for survival and execution.

The language that we developed was born on African soil as a pidgin, an auxiliary language. As in case with pidgins, it was developed for communication purposes, spoken among various African groups in business transactions and intertribal affairs. By the height of the slave trade, pidgins were firmly placed among African groups. When different Africans were captured and housed together in West Coast holding cells, the pidgins spoken in freedom, became their method of communication in captivity.

As time went on, the main auxiliary language combined the most prominent pidgins, other linguistics features and speech patterns common among them with the English words and vocabulary spoken to and about them by the master class. This creolization set the stage, on African soil, for what is now still spoken and called Gullah. It was sustained because of the large numbers of Africans on rice and Sea Island cotton plantations, the isolation that characterized the regions along the coast and the continued influx of pure Africans smuggled into these isolated areas after the slave trade was prohibited.

The lanuage as it exists today still contains African words and language features that can be traced to African groups today. The absence of the verb to be, final *t's* , and the use of only two pronouns *'e* (he, she it) and *onna* (you, us, them) bears witness to the fact that what ever its history, the Gullah language has its own flavor, rules and regulations.

Gullah Food

Gullah Food is older than the South and as ancient as the world. It is one of the oldest African and

American traditions being practiced in this country today. As it has always been, it is informed by need, availability and environment. The Africans brought to the Carolina colony used the similarities between culinary environments of the low country and the West Coast of Africa to create a food culture that has come to characterize the regions where they live.

One of the biggest ironies is that rice, the grain that had been in African food culture for thousands of years, became the cash crop and reason for the American enslavement of many Gullah people.

For years, the oceans, other bodies of water, and farming practices remained in the backdrop while rice, seafood and vegetables (corn, sweet potatoes, tomatoes, collards, turnips, peanuts, okra, eggplant, beans and peas) brought the connection between both sides of the Atlantic full circle. Slave cooks simply adapted their African cooking traditions to American soil.

Even today, cooking traditions remain somewhat consistent. One pot dishes, deep frying, rice dishes, sea food, boiling and steaming, baking in ashes, basic and natural seasonings, and food types consistent with those received in the weekly rations on plantations are all characteristics of Gullah food.

The food is characterized by the ever presence of rice and a distinct "taste" present wherever Gullah people are cooking. The recipes are simply frames; the art work is created in the taste buds of the preparer. Try to obtain a recipe or cooking directions from Gullah cooks, and you will more than likely get the generic response, "ah 'on measur." They will tell you that they cook "cordin' ta taste." This taste is passed down from generation to generation, but unlike other ingredients, it is an elusive quality guided by memory and taste buds, almost impossible to explain in words. It is an ingredient that must be experienced. Tasted first, then duplicated each time Gullah food is prepared.

Under the task system used on most rice plantations, each slave was assigned a certain task each day. These tasks included ground breaking, digging trenches, plowing, hoeing, harrowing, threshing and other specific tasks related to rice farming. Unlike gang labor employed on cotton and tobacco plantations, when slaves on rice plantations finished their assigned tasks, they were generally free to tend their own gardens, fish or hunt for wild game. As a consequence, they were often able to enhance and supplement their ration supply with vegetables from their own gardens, natural seasonings, wild game, chicken, eggs and fish. These supplements also include leftovers given to them during hog killings. Feet, ears, entrails, jowls, heads and the like are still favorite meats for celebrations.

Slave cooks simply incorporated the weekly rations given to slave families into the African cooking traditions of their ancestors. A glance at the average food ration given on Brookgreen Plantation in Murrells Inlet in the 1800's reads like a grocery list for a 21st century household.

Simply speaking, Gullah food is about ancestral ties and American living, adaptability, creativity, making do, livin' ot da waddah and on the lan'. It is a culture within the culture, with its own history, heritage, and distinction. It is a food culture handed down through practice more so than with words It lives among us in the restaurants, homes, kitchens, backyards, family reunions, church anniversaries, birthday parties and other celebrations that dot across the grounds that the Gullah call home

Gullah Art

Gullah art is distinctly African. Enslaved Africans and those Gullah who lived in the period of isolation that followed Emancipation, made a wide assortment of artifacts bearing great similarity to West African art; wooden mortars and pestles, rice "farmers," clay pots, calabash containers, baskets, palm leaf brooms, drums, and hand-woven cotton blankets dyed with indigo. Gullah men continue the tradition of wood carving, making elaborate grave monuments, human figures, and walking sticks. Gullah women sew quilts organized in strips like African country cloth, and keep the tradition of the sweetgrass basket making alive today, especially in the Mount Pleasant community just outside of Charleston, South Carolina.

Gullah painting is traditionally very vibrant and colorful with subjects typically centered around community life, as is very evident in the works of Jonathan Green and Diane Britton Dunham.

Gullah Crafts

Perhaps nothing is as representative of a Gullah craft as the iconic sweetgrass basket. This exquisite art form was brought to the lowcountry of South Carolina in the 17th century by enslaved Africans from West Africa; primarily from the regions today referred to as the Mano River Region, Senegambia and Agola-Congolesse.

Early basket making in the United States went *hand in glove* with rice cultivation on the Southeastern coast and the intricate network of plantations. It is noteworthy that typically enslaved African men made the baskets and basket making was often relegated to the men who were no longer able to work the fields due to age or infirmity.

After Emancipation sweetgrass baskets transformed from the larger baskets used in rice cultivation to small baskets made by women. These smaller baskets were used in various environments for storing and serving food and this is believed to have been the turning point from an agricultural craft to a collectable art form.

Gullah Music

The roots of the Gullah culture began in Sierra Leone, Gambia, Senegal, and Angola. Of the many influences that came from this region, music played a major role. African songs and the foundation from which they came are deeply rooted in what evolved into Negro spirituals, slave songs, and now celebrated as Gullah music. You will also find Gullah influence in Jazz and Blues.

Perhaps most famously, the Gullah culture produced two iconic songs; "Michael Row the Boat Ashore (or Michael Row Your Boat Ashore) believed to have been written about a slave who would row his mistress across Beaufort Bay, and "Kum Bah Yah," a phrase which is in the Gullah dialect.

Traditional Gullah music makes use of hand-clapping, foot-stomping, gourds with seeds (not unlike maracas) and African drums, but typically no other instruments.

The Gullah Kinfolk have perfected this musical style and revel in keeping tradition alive.

Gullah Religion

In early times, Christianity was used to justify both slavery and abolition. In pre-Civil War times, African Americans could not get together for fear of insurrection. Many would gather late at night and out of site, to pray in the heavy brush. These places of worship were originally known as "Hush Harbors" and later became "the invisible church."

Hand clapping, foot stopping and ring shouts of adoration and praise were common forms of religious expression, but in extreme cases where secrecy was critical for worship, enslaved Africans put their lips on the ground to muffle their words and ensure the master and overseer would not hear them.

Praising God was a day to day, hour to hour, minute to minute, communion with the creator; not relegated to only one day per week.

Travel and Tourism

Hilton Head Island is known far and wide as a vacation destination that prides itself on its top-notch golf courses and tennis programs, world-class resorts, and beautiful beaches. But the island is also part of the storied American South, steeped in a rich, colorful history. It has seen Native Americans and explorers, battles from the Revolutionary War to the Civil War, plantations and slaves, and development and environmentally focused growth.

More than 10,000 years ago, the island was inhabited by Paleo-Indians. From 8000 to 2000 BC, Woodland Indians lived on the island. A shell ring made from their discarded oyster shells and animal bones from that period can be found in the Sea Pines Nature Preserve.

The recorded history of the island goes back to the early 1500s, when Spanish explorers sailing coastal waters came upon the island and found Native American settlements. Over the next 200 years, the island was claimed at various times by the Spanish, the French, and the British. In 1663, Captain William Hilton claimed the island for the British crown (and named it for himself), and the island became home to indigo, rice, and cotton plantations.

During the Revolutionary War, the British harassed islanders and burned plantations. During the War of 1812, British troops again burned plantations, but the island recovered from both wars. During the Civil War, Union troops took Hilton Head in

1861 and freed the more than 1,000 slaves on the island. Mitchelville, one of the first settlements for freed blacks, was created. There was no bridge to the island, so its freed slaves, called "Gullah," subsisted on agriculture and the seafood-laden waters.

Over the years, much of the plantation land was sold at auction. Then, in 1949, General Joseph Fraser purchased 17,000 acres, much of which would eventually become various communities, including Hilton Head Plantation, Palmetto Dunes, and Spanish Wells. The general bought another 1,200 acres, which his son, Charles, used to develop Sea Pines. The first bridge to the island was built in 1956, and modern-day Hilton Head was born.

What makes Hilton Head so special now? Charles Fraser and his business associates focused on development while preserving the environment. And that is what tourists will see today: an island that values its history and its natural beauty.

Hilton Head Island visitor guide
Vacation Arrangements

Making Special Arrangements for your Hilton Head vacation

Pets

The best bet is to leave your pets at home. If you must bring a pet, ask the rental agent for an accommodation that will accept pets. This will narrow your choices to a very few properties. A few motels accept pets. You can bring your pet and board it at some of the veterinary clinics or at the Evergreen Pet Lodge, and on the Internet you can find some private rental homes that will take in dogs.

Most condominium associations have banned pets even for property owners. If you try to sneak a pet in, chances are you will be noticed and reported. This could result in eviction.

Rental equipment

Hilton Head Outfitters rents Surf boards, beach umbrellas and chairs, paddleboards, fishing rods and jogging strollers. Keen's Beach Rentals rents beach stuff including coolers. Hilton Head Bike Rentals has a wide selection of items, from bikes to beds to beach and baby stuff.

Baby Needs

Baby furniture such as high chairs, cribs, playpens and strollers can be rented through your rental agent or supplied by your hotel. If you plan ahead these items can be placed in your accommodation before your arrival and picked up after your departure. For sanitary reasons, crib sheets are sometimes not provided - play it safe and bring one. Baby's Away, Hilton Head Baby Rental, and many bike rental companies (ask for a package deal) rent baby gear.

Audio & Video Equipment

You can expect one TV and maybe a VCR in a hotel. Rental villas often have more - ask before you lug that heavy stuff with you. These items can also be rented, however TV reception is not possible by antenna alone, so a TV is of little use without a cable jack. Some villas have CD players and stereos, but this is not the norm.

Computer Access

If you leave your computer at home, you can still have access to a PC at The UPS Store. The cost is $15.00 per hour with a $5.00 minimum. They also have copiers and all kinds of office services. 843-842-3171.

If you just want to check your e-mail, the Public Library will provide access for only $2/Hr, though there may be a wait to get on their computers.

Ask your rental agent if they can provide access for checking e-mail.

If you want to go on line with your own computer.

Boats

Hilton Head has several boat launching ramps, so bringing a boat for day use is complicated only by the need to store it and its trailer overnight. Some hotels have parking areas for boat trailers. Rental houses usually can accommodate trailers, but condos cannot. There are several storage companies (the kind that have the sheds) that accept boats and trailers. Some of them are:

U Store It 843-681-7212 (mid island) and 843-681-4130 (mid island) and Beach City Self Storage 843-681-7333 (mid island). A new public access boat launching ramp opened August 1, 2005 in Broad Creek at the Cross Island Expressway bridge.

Access is from Helmsman's Way. It will provide deep water access and includes a floating dock. Another public access ramp, Broad Creek Landing, is on Marshland Rd. but it can be iffy at low tide. You can launch at some of our marinas. There are several ramps in neighboring Bluffton and one on Pinckney Island.

If you have a boat you want to launch on arrival and keep in the water, you need to contact a local marina to make arrangements. Not all marinas will be able to accommodate, and some may sell out of space in the summer.

Vehicles

Hilton Head has limited parking facilities, so some properties restrict the number of vehicles a renter can park. Most hotels do not have a problem, but if you are staying in a condo or house and have more than two vehicles, make sure they can be accommodated.

Motorcycles are prohibited in almost all plantations (noise) and some condominiums and timeshares.

Vehicles with signage on them are restricted in some places, especially from overnight parking.

If you bring any kind of trailer, make arrangements or plan to put it in a storage facility, such as: U Store It 843-681-7212 (mid island) and 843-681-4130 (mid island) and Beach City Self Storage 843-681-7333 (mid island).

Motor Homes

There are two motor home parking facilities on Hilton Head. No motor homes (or tents or anything else) are permitted on the beach overnight if at all. Outdoor Resorts, at the south end of the island can accommodate a motor home for $57 to $77 per day, renting space owned by individuals. Outdoor RV Resort and Marina, at the north end does also for $49 to $64 per night. Motor homes can be stored at many of the commercial storage facilities such as: U Store It 843-681-7212 (mid island) and 843-681-4130 (mid island) and Beach City Self Storage 843-681-7333 (mid island).

Handicapped Access and Equipment

Many properties on Hilton Head were built before ADA and are not well equipped to handle handicapped visitors. This is not to say it's impossible, just that planning ahead is essential. If you rent a home or condo, let the rental agent know if you cannot negotiate stairs - there are plenty of single story properties available. Most hotels are OK, but some motels will need to know your needs. Wheelchair mats have been added to all beaches to permit wheelchairs to cross the loose sand to firmer sand.

Equipment such as wheelchairs, oxygen systems, and other aids can be rented from Burke's Main Street Pharmacy and other places.

Bicycles

Hilton Head Island is very flat, and with parking limited in some areas, bikes are a great way to get around. Beach bikes rent for about $25 per week (ask for multiple bike discounts) including helmet and chain lock. You can bring your own, but the salt air is rough on bikes and you can't take them inside your rental property to keep them safe. During low tide, our beaches are very firm and you can easily ride a bike with wide tires on the beach.

You can also rent bikes by the day or even by the hour. For those with children, there are tandem bikes (built for two - one adult, one child), kiddy trailers, training wheels, and kiddy seats (behind the adult). For those who have never ridden a bike, there are adult tricycles. There are even jitney bikes that hold four to six people.

South Carolina law permits bikes on all roadways. They must adhere to the same traffic laws as motor vehicles, including riding <u>with</u> the traffic, but as far to the right as practical. The leisure trails are much safer. There are 57 miles of "leisure" trails on the island that accommodate bikes, with 28 additional miles in progress, and more inside the gated communities. Bikes on leisure trails must yield to traffic at intersections and driveways, which is where most accidents occur.

During the busy season it's a good idea to reserve bikes ahead of time. Ask the rental company what their policy is regarding stolen bikes. There are some people who like to take a bike at night for a joy ride and then abandon it. Usually they are recovered, but most rental companies will hold you financially responsible for the value of the bike.

When you arrive on the island, go to the bike rental company and pick out your bikes and have them adjusted for you. The bike rental company will deliver them to your accommodation and pick them up the day you leave at no extra charge.

Welcome Gifts

Someone you know on a honeymoon or other special occasion? Their hotel or rental agent will be glad to deliver a gift basket of fruit, candies, wine, cheese, or whatever goodies you desire to the guest at your request. Other sources include florists and Wine & Cheese if You Please. If you don't have their rental property address, you can have gifts delivered to their rental agent. Or you can telephone a restaurant and with your credit card arrange for a gift certificate that can be picked up at the door.

Geography of Hilton Head Island

Hilton Head Island is a barrier island off the coast of South Carolina, located about 30 highway miles north of Savannah, GA. At seven miles in width and fourteen in length, it is the second largest Atlantic coast barrier island after Long Island, NY.

It is shaped roughly like a tennis sneaker, with the "toe" known as the south end, the "ball" of the foot is Forest Beach, and the "top" is the north end.

Hilton Head Island is almost bisected by Broad Creek, which is navigable for most of its length and is home to several marinas.

The island is separated from the mainland by the Calibogue sound and the Intracoastal Waterway. Between Hilton Head and the mainland are two islands. Daufuskie island is accessible only by water and is partly wild and partly developed for tourism. Pinckney island is accessible from the bridge linking Hilton Head to the mainland, and it is a National Wildlife Refuge popular among bird watchers.

On Hilton Head are several "plantations", which are private, gated communities with restricted access. All beaches on Hilton Head are public, though access from the interior may be restricted. There are many miles of beach, making it easy to get away from crowded "hot spots". Dunes separate the beach from the interior, and provide protection against storm surges. The ecological balance of the dunes is very delicate, so crossing them is permitted only at boardwalk-like walkovers. The width of the beach is affected by tides, which commonly run eight feet. Keep this in mind when you leave a towel or shoes at low tide - eight feet of tide translates to many yards of beach. The beach slopes very gradually into the ocean, which limits waves to less than surfing size. There are some areas of beach that can have treacherous currents during tidal changes. No motor vehicles are permitted on the beaches.

A four lane highway, US 278, (William Hilton Parkway) runs the length of Hilton Head, from the bridge to the south end. The cross island expressway is a toll road that provides a shortcut from the north end to the south end. The $1.25 toll is well worth the 12 traffic lights and four miles it cuts out (you'll save that in gasoline). US 278 ends at Sea Pines circle, the same place you will end up if you use the expressway. From the circle Pope Avenue takes you to the beach at Coligny circle, and South Forest Beach Drive runs along the ocean from there.

There is no "downtown" on Hilton Head. Shopping and activities are spread throughout, although more heavily concentrated on the south end of the island. We have no malls.

Weather in Hilton Head is semi-tropical. In winter temperatures rarely drop below freezing. In the summer it can get quite hot, with July and August highs occasionally reaching 100 degrees. On hot summer days, tropical afternoon thundershowers are common, though not long lasting. They are usually accompanied by potentially dangerous lightning. If you are caught outside get off the beach and stay away from tall trees. Visitors are sometimes surprised by the intensity of the sun and have their vacation spoiled by sunburn. Please be cautious - it's no fun spending part of your vacation in your room in discomfort.

What to do in Hilton Head Islad

Hilton Head Beaches

Hilton Heads 14 miles of beach is mostly along the Atlantic Ocean coast, some is along the Calibogue Sound, some on the Port Royal Sound at Port Royal plantation and Hilton Head plantation has a small beach next to Dolphin Head, also on Port Royal sound. The newly opened Fish Haul Creek Park offers a little known beach access to a beach on the Port Royal Sound. The beach there is quite private (no, not <u>that</u> private) but with little wave action.

Along the beach you will see numbered markers which have been put in place to help identify the location to emergency responders. The numbers start at "one" on the Calibogue beach at Lands End in Sea Pines plantation and increment by one every tenth of a mile as you go North or East. Numbers ending in "A" "B" or "C" designate a location between the two numbers on either side and are not indicative of miles..

The beaches slope very gradually in most areas. You can go out a long way from shore and still be able to stand with your head above water (there are some places where tidal currents produce deep holes, so be careful). This gradual slope inhibits wave action, so Hilton Head is not a place to surfboard unless you are just learning. It also means the tides have a very significant effect on the width of the beach. When the tide is high, there is still a good beach from approximately beach marker 80A to Tower Beach in Sea Pines, at beach marker 13 and even as far as marker 8, and also from marker 102 to 111A. Depending on how high the tide is and when the last beach renourishment took place, other locations may prove unusable at high tide.

The sand below the mid tide line is usually hard packed enough to support a bicycle with wide tires, and biking on the beach at or near low tide is a popular pastime (you should be warned that hitting a patch of soft sand will bring you to a very sudden stop). Beach bikers have learned to check the wind direction before heading out - riding into the wind is like riding uphill, and vice versa.

There are seven "public access"[1] beach areas popular with visitors (most are attended by life guards from Memorial weekend to Labor Day). Pay parking is available at all but the Islander's Beach Park, and there are reserved parking spots for those who purchase annual beach tags (available to Hilton Head property owners only).

Alder Lane

The southern most of these beach access locations is beside the Marriott Grand Ocean Resort on South Forest Beach Rd. at Alder Lane. There is parking across South Forest Beach Rd at the meters for 25¢ for 15 minutes. This is a nice wide beach and is relatively uncrowded. Amenities include restrooms and a drink vending machine. It's an easy bike ride from most south end locations. This beach also is equipped with the mats that make it wheelchair accessible.

Burke's Beach
Burke's Beach is located off William Hilton parkway (278 Bus.) at Burke's Beach Rd. The parking is very limited, though you can park next door at Chaplin Park. There are no amenities. A reader recently reported there is now a lifeguard there. There is no beach matting for wheelchair access. This beach is very uncrowded. Thanks, Pat M.

Coligny Beach

This beach is located at Coligny circle at Pope Avenue and South Forest Beach Drive. It's the island's busiest beach, in part because volleyball nets are available and an outdoor bar is located just off the beach at the Holiday Inn. There are rest rooms, changing rooms, water fountains, sand showers, pay telephones and other amenities. Mats designed to make the beach wheelchair accessible are at this location. Life Guards rent beach equipment, Hobie Cats, recumbent bikes, sand trikes, umbrellas, etc.

 Parking is available at the town parking lot at the corner of South Forest Beach Drive and Pope Avenue. The entrance is on Pope across from the Exxon. It costs $4.00 for the day ($2.00 after 2:00 PM), with in and out privileges (keep your receipt). There is also parking closer to the beach, on Coligny Circle on the North side, but it fills up quickly. Coligny Plaza, adjacent, offers many shops and eaterires. Please don't park in the Plaza to go to the beach - the merchants don't appreciate it and your vehicle could be towed.

Though this beach can become crowded in season, you have only to walk a few hundred yards North or South to get away from the crowds.

Dreissen Beach Park (Singleton Beach)

Dreissen beach is also off William Hilton parkway, at Bradley Beach Rd. It has Life Guards, plenty of parking, rest rooms, sand showers and vending machines. It has a playground and a few picnic tables, one with a grill nearby. The boardwalk to the beach is quite long and requires healthy legs. If you park here, note the number of your parking space and go to the machine at the building housing the restrooms to pay. It takes quarters. This beach is equipped with the mats that make it wheelchair accessible.

Folly Field Beach

Folly Field beach is located on Starfish Road, a right turn off Folly Field Road. Parking is somewhat limited (52 spaces at meters at 25¢ per 15 minute period), but restrooms, sand showers, Life Guards and water fountains are available. While dangerous conditions such as riptides and undertows can exist on any beach, the Folly is an area where swimmers have (rarely) gotten in trouble. This beach also is equipped with the mats that make it wheelchair accessible. It is the favorite beach for surfers.

Fish Haul Creek Park
(Mitchelville Beach Park)

The beach is accessed from the park and is a considerable walk from it. The beach is on Port Royal Sound with not much wave action, but it is a little used beach, often deserted, and very wide at low tide. If privacy is your bag, you might want to check it out.

Islander's Beach Club

As the name implies, this beach is intended primarily for locals. Parking is available only for those who purchase annual permits, which are limited to Hilton Head property owners. There is nothing other than that to keep visitors from enjoying this beach park - you can always have someone drop you off or go by bike. Amenities here include restrooms, changing rooms, playground, soft drink machine, sand showers and a few picnic tables. It's located off Folly Field Road at Sparkleberry Lane (actual address is 94 Folly Field Rd.). This beach also is equipped with the mats that make it wheelchair accessible.

Other Beaches, South to North
South Beach

In Sea Pines plantation, at the "toe" of the island

near the South Beach marina, is the Calibogue beach. There is no public parking, so walking or biking are indicated. There are two characteristics of this beach area that are of interest : at high tide there is little or no beach; and tidal currents will move you up or down the beach depending on flow. There are no amenities here. Otherwise, this is a pleasant and uncrowded area where dolphins and other wildlife abound.

Tower Beach

Tower Beach is located in Sea Pines plantation on the Atlantic ocean. This beach is <u>intended</u> for use by property owners, and parking is restricted to property owners, though it is otherwise accessible to anyone by bicycle or on foot. It provides restrooms, water fountains, and a picnic area with barbeque grills.

Sea Pines Beach Club

This beach is also in Sea Pines plantation on the Atlantic ocean. It offers many amenities such as restrooms, food service, a bar, picnic tables, showers, entertainment and activities for children (seasonal). It is attended by lifeguards and has some parking, which fills up quickly in season. The Sea Pines trolley provides transportation to the Beach Club from the Greenwood Drive parking lot, Harbour Town and other locations. Parking at this beach is available to anyone staying in Sea Pines.

Crown Plaza Resort

This beach is in Shipyard plantation and is accessible to those staying in Shipyard. Parking is available at the very end of Shipyard Drive, though it fills up in the busy season. Visitors to the Crown Plaza can also enjoy this beach, but consider access through the hotel to be for hotel guests only.

Palmetto Dunes Beach

In the vicinity of the Marriott Beach and Golf Resort, this beach is accessible to guests staying in Palmetto Dunes plantation and can also be enjoyed by visitors to the hotel. There is a pleasant ocean front bar at the hotel from where the beach can be admired.

Westin Resort Hotel

This beach is accessible primarily through the hotel, which is limited to hotel guests. It is only a few hundred feet from the Islander Beach Club (see above).

Beach Regulations

The beach regulations are posted all along the beach. For the most part they are logical rules designed to ensure a safe and enjoyable experience for those using the beach. For example, there are restrictions regarding playing Frisbee, flying stunt kites and fishing in "designated swimming areas" (those listed above) because these are activities that could cause injury to those on a crowded beach. The regulations are enforced by the lifeguards and sheriff's deputies.

Four regulations you might not expect are:

No alcoholic beverages are permitted on any part of the beach.

You may not beach a power craft (including wave runners) on any beach , and they must be operated more than 150 Yards offshore, for the protection of swimmers.

You may not walk on the sand dunes, as they are very fragile and are our protection against storm surge from gales and hurricanes.

You may not remove any living creature from the beach (hermit crabs, starfish, sand dollars, etc.). What you think is a shell could be a hermit crab's home.

And, there is something we locals would ask of you: Take nothing but your memories, leave nothing but your footprints.

Dogs love the beach, but not everyone loves dogs (some people fear them). Consequently there are rules regarding dogs on the beach. The rules vary depending on the time of year. Few vacationers bring dogs because it's difficult to find housing that will accept pets, but if you bring your dog, make sure you are aware of the restrictions. Above all, pick up after your pet. Be aware joggers are common on the beach and dogs like to chase them.

Beach Amenities

The lifeguards on Hilton Head get paid based on commissions on rentals of beach chairs, umbrellas, recumbent beach bicycles, hobie cats, and water tricycles. You can rent any of these and more right on the beach. A "set" of two chairs and an umbrella rent for $27.00 the first day and $16.00 on subsequent days if paid in advance (2003 rates). The company involved is called Shore Beach Services and their phone number is 843-785-3494. You might want to try some of the companies that rent bikes, cribs, etc. for chair and umbrella prices. Several companies rent beach equipment at very competitive prices

A bike ride down the Atlantic beach

If you bike from the Westin or Islander Beach Park to Land's End in Sea Pines, you will have traveled about 11 miles one way. You can do this on a beach bike in an hour and a half with the wind at your back if you don't stop. But, it will be much more enjoyable if you make some stops and learn about the island from the beach, even if you don't make the whole trip. Let's take a hypothetical bike excursion. With the wind at our backs, and a couple of hours before low tide, we start at:

The Islander Beach Club, at beach marker *110* (11 miles from marker 1) and head south.

Within a few hundred feet we see a large complex of high rise, brown, wood buildings. This is Hilton Head Beach and Tennis Resort, a budget priced tourist accommodation. There is a bar beachside, and although this is private property they might not mind serving up a cool one or feeding you. There is entertainment in season..

At marker *105* (you have now traveled all of a half mile) is Folly Field Beach Park, described above. Not much to do here unless you need to use the restrooms. While dangerous conditions such as riptides and undertows can exist on any beach, the Folly is an area where swimmers have gotten in trouble.

Marker *102* is where the Dreissen Beach Park is located (description above). If you have children with you, they can enjoy the playground or you can break out the sandwiches and sit at a picnic table.

At marker *98* is Burke's Beach. Not much to do here except watch people crabbing in the estuarine creeks.

At marker 94A you might want to stop in at Coco's On the Beach for a cold one.

Marker *82* is the Marriott Beach and Golf Resort in Palmetto Dunes Plantation. Here is the Point Comfort poolside and beachside bar, and Quinn's II, a restaurant offering a limited menu of good food at either outdoor tables or inside in the air conditioning, also with an ocean view.

Disney Resort, the time share at Shelter Cove, has a beachfront facility at marker *80A* just past marker 81.

The next hotel you will see is the Crown Plaza Resort in Shipyard Plantation at marker *71A,* just past marker 72. This hotel has a poolside bar, but it's located a fairly long walk from the beach through a pavilion used for group affairs. The bar hours are a mystery to me, but the grounds are quite attractive.

Now we have a stretch of about a mile before we hit the busiest part of the beach, starting at mile 61, where the Sea Crest has an ocean front bar and food service between their two swimming pools.

Immediately past the Sea Crest at marker 59A is Coligny Beach, the island's most popular, described above. Right next to it is the Holiday Inn's Tiki Hut, a popular beach bar that offers entertainment afternoons and evenings in season. The public is always welcome at the Tiki Hut.

Less than a mile further you will see the Marriott Grand Ocean Resort, a high rise time share. Immediately next to it is the Alder Lane public beach, at marker 52A. You can get a soft drink from a vending machine there or use the restrooms, because the next segment is a mile and a half away.

At marker 38 is the popular Sea Pines Beach Club, described above. Here you can stop for a drink, a burger, and to listen to some entertainment.

The next mile and a half is my favorite stretch of beach. It's very wide and lined with impressive mansions. Wildlife is ever present - Ospreys diving for their catch, Dolphins rising to breathe or slapping the water with their tails to stun fish, and entertaining Pelicans doing their ungainly crash dives. At marker 13 is Tower Beach. Not much reason to stop here unless you need to use the restrooms.

The next mile or so takes you around the "toe" of Hilton Head, a turn toward the West. The beach here is Calibogue Sound beach, and it also teems with wildlife. If the timing is right, you might see a great sunset here. The beach ends at a breakwater that slows the migration of sand into the mouth of Braddock Cove, the entrance to the South Beach marina. In the distance you can see the Harbour Town lighthouse, and on your right is Land's End, a South Beach community.

That's the end of our hypothetical trip. Since Sea Pines plantation is private, and, since going from the beach inland is technically trespassing, we might want to double back to where we can legally get back to the street. To do this you need to go back beyond the Sea Pines Beach Club, perhaps to Alder Lane at marker 53. I certainly would not advocate trespassing and bringing the bikes in at marker 4, where the catamarans and other boats are beached if you are not staying in the plantation. By now the tide is coming in and we can ride back along the leisure trails, where the wind is much less noticeable.

[1] *All beaches on Hilton Head are public. "Public access" means you can get to the beach without entering private property. If you are staying in a plantation, you are welcome to access the beach from their property. If you are not staying in a plantation, you can still use the beach adjacent to the plantation as long as you get to it by walking or biking along the beach. Yes, it's a silly distinction.*

Tennis on Hilton Head Island

Hilton Head is a tennis players dream come true. There are hundreds of courts all over the island, and several clubs rated in Tennis Magazine's top 50 clubs. Hilton Head is also home to two famous tennis pros: Dennis Van der Meer and Stan Smith. The Van der Meer tennis university is world renown for teaching both amateurs and professionals. Add to that a mild climate that makes the season almost year around , the availability of all three Grand Slam playing surfaces and accessibility of lighted courts for night play and you have a tennis paradise.

Some residential developments have their own courts, which may be used by guests staying in those developments. Most players go to one of the public courts listed below. Click on the green ones to go to their web site.

CLUB	COURTS	TELEPHONE

Palmetto Dunes Tennis Center	23 clay, 2 Nova ProBounce (6 lighted) 8 Pickle Ball	843-785-1152
Port Royal Racquet Club	10 Har-tru, 4 Nova Some lighted	843-686-8803
Sea Pines Racquet Club	23 clay	843-363-4495
Shipyard Racquet Club (Van der Meer)	13 Har-Tru, 7 hard, 8 lighted, 3 indoor	843-686-8804
South Beach Racquet Club	13 clay, 2 lighted.	843-671-2215
Van der Meer Tennis Center	17 hard, 4 covered and lighted	843-785-8388

Van der Meer has daily adult programs and round robins at Shipyard.

There are 6 public tennis courts on Hilton Head Island under the supervision of the Island Recreation Center and with the cooperation of Public Tennis, Inc. All are lighted for night play. They are at the Chaplin Public Tennis Center in the

Chaplin Community Park off Burkes Beach road. They are available on a first come, first served basis.

From Memorial Day to Labor Day fees are charged for the use of these courts (contrary to the belief of some real estate agents). They are open from 8:00 AM to 9:30 PM unless reserved for lessons or USTA use. For more information call Cameron Everett at 843-681-7273.

Two courts are available at the Old Schoolhouse park on the north end. They are under the supervision of the Beaufort County Parks and Leisure Services.

Hilton Head High School has six courts and Hilton Head Middle School four more which are available weekend and evenings when school is in session and anytime in the summer. These courts have no user fees.

Hilton Head Island Golf

Golf is a favorite sport on Hilton Head, which offers 15 public access courses on the island and nine more nearby. This is an overview of the courses which includes some specifications and price ranges. Prices for golf are seasonal, and change at different times for the various courses. Prices are also subject to "specials" offered by the courses, often reflecting <u>discounts</u> for afternoon play or to play multiple courses. The rules for making tee times vary among the courses as well.

We suggest you discuss your golf requirements with the provider of your accommodations, and request a tee time be made for your first day, at least. This will give you an opportunity to check out availability at other courses without missing a day of golf.

Most hotels and rental agencies can provide a golf package, including the cost of accommodations and play at <u>discount</u> rates. Packages can be for a week or less, and can include any number of golfers. You should make sure the provider of accommodations understands the makeup of your party so suitable accommodations are provided. For example, if your group is all men, you should make clear you expect a separate bed for each person.

Golf lessons are available at most golf courses. Whether you are just beginning to play the game or have been playing for years, our PGA Professionals can help you in every aspect of your game. Discounts available to guests of Seashore Vacations, Inc. Junior golfers can learn at the International Junior Golf Academy.

Heron Point is the new name of the Sea Pines Ocean Course following extensive remodeling. It was designed by Pete Dye and it opened September 15, 2007.

Public Courses on Hilton head island

Course	Location	Length (Yds.)	Par	Rating	Slope	2007 Price Range	Phone
Country Club of Hilton Head	Hilton Head Plantation	6162	72	70.6	129	$79 to $105	866-699-6391
Oyster Reef	Hilton Head Plantation	6071	72	71.0	121	$55 to $107	843-681-1750
Golden Bear	Indigo Run Plantation	5259 (6 tees)	72	66.4	115	$72 to $92	843-689-2200
Robert Trent Jones	Palmetto Dunes	6122	72	69.1	122	$78 to $148	843-785-1138
George Fazio Course	Palmetto Dunes	6239	70	70.2	126	$64 to $114	843-785-1138
Arthur Hills Course	Palmetto Dunes	6122	72	70.4	125	$74 to $128	843-785-

							1138
Arthur Hills Course	Palmetto Hall Plantation	6257	72	71.0	127	$65 to $107	843-689-4100
Robert Cupp Course	Palmetto Hall Plantation	6042	72	69.2	125	$61 to $108	843-689-4100
Planter's Row	Port Royal Plantation	5920	72	68.7	129	$49 to $99	843-689-4653
Robber's Row	Port Royal Plantation	6011	72	70.3	116	$49 to $99	843-689-4653
Barony Course	Port Royal Plantation	5964	72	69.0	122	$49 to $99	843-689-4653
Harbour Town Golf Links	Sea Pines Plantation	6040	71	69.9	130	$195 to $260	843-842-8484
Heron Point	Sea Pines Plantation	7 tees 7103 to 3743	71	75.4-66.4	143-112	$110 to $140	843-842-8484
Ocean Course	Sea Pines Plantation	6172	72	70.4	123	$80 to $130	843-842-8484
Shipyard Golf Club[1]	Shipyard Plantation	varies		varies	varies	$58 to $97	843-681-1750

Nearby public courses

Course	Location	Length (Yds.)	Par	Rating	Slope	Price Range	Phone
Rose Hill Golf Club	Bluffton	8 tees	36	varies	varies	$55 to $65	843-757-9030
Old South	Bluffton	5779	72	69.3	120	$70 to $80	843-785-5353
Okatie Creek	Sun City	5955 (5 tees)	72	68.8	117	$37 to $42	843-705-4653
Hidden Cypress	Sun City	5974 (6 tees)	72	68.9	118	$37 to $42	843-705-4999
Argent Lakes	Sun City		61			$28 to $34	843-645-0507
Island West	Bluffton	6208	72	70.1	127	$30 to $33	843-689-6660
Hilton Head National	Bluffton	5628	71	67.4	119	$50 to $80	843-842-5900
Eagle's Point	Bluffton	6026	71		117	$59 to	843-686-

Golf Club				68.2		$79	4457
Crescent Point Golf Club	Bluffton	5987	71	69.6	128	$49 to $72	843-706-2600
The IX @ Old Carolina	Bluffton	3075	36/35	35.1	126		843-757-8311

General note: Some clubs are reserved for member play only at certain times. All clubs reserve the right to change prices without notice - confirm when you reserve tee times.

Note [1]: Shipyard has three 9-hole courses. Golfers play two (or three) of them.

Some courses offer 9 hole rates. Some low end rates quoted are for 3 day packages or require a coupon.

Nature

Few places can compete with Hilton Head for nature lovers. Wildlife abounds on land, in lagoons and in the ocean. We hope this page will help you enjoy observing our wildlife. If you are a nature lover, check with the Coastal Discovery Museum to see what their programs for nature walks, kayaking, and bird watching are (689-6767). They are in Honey Horn Plantation. Another wonderful source of more detailed information is the book Tideland Treasures, by Todd Ballantine, a local naturalist. The book is available at most bookstores - the last copy I bought was $12 - and at some drugstores. It's one you will want to take home.

Birds

It is an oversimplification to divide birds into the categories of shore birds and inland birds, but it helps in identification. Generally, shore birds have long legs for their bodies because they feed by wading in the water and eating fish or small crustaceans. The smallest are Piping Plovers, which can be seen running along the tide line so fast their legs are a blur. Somewhat larger, but of similar behavior, are Sanderlings and Sandpipers. Egrets are found more often in lagoons and marshes than on the beach. These are the large, pure white, long legged birds with a very long skinny neck. The Great White Egret is the larger one, distinguished by a yellow beak. The smaller Snowy Egret has a black beak. During nesting season both these birds display beautiful, long, delicate plumes. The huge grayish blue birds similar to Egrets are Great Blue Herons. They can be seen in lagoons and marshes, but they do come to the beach at dusk and often remain until nightfall.

Some other long-legged birds you might see are:

The Ibis, often found on golf courses and identified by a long, curved beak. The Ibis is white when mature, but youngsters are mostly brown.

The Wood Stork, becoming more common on Hilton Head as they lose habitat in Florida. This bird looks all white when it's on land, but reveals half black wings (underside) when flying. The Wood Stork is endangered, with a declining population, due to wetlands drainage in Florida. At this time they are headed toward certain extinction.

The cattle Egret can be found in horse pastures. This is a small white Egret, with some brown accents on its head, breast and back.

Brown Pelicans are entertaining to watch. They glide gracefully through the air, often skimming along inches above the water. As graceful as they are when flying, they are ungainly when feeding. A

Pelican will hover about 30 feet above the water looking for small fish, then suddenly fold its wings and crash unceremoniously into the water to grab its prey.

The dark colored birds standing with their wings outstretched are either Anhingas or Cormorants. Cormorants are more common and can be identified by a hooked beak, whereas the Anhinga has a straight, pointed beak. These birds feed by swimming under water, which they do very well. They are often seen in the water, with little more than their long neck above the surface, hence their nickname, snakebird. You might see a Common Loon, which looks like the Anhinga or Cormorant but has a shorter neck and is much more rare (declining population).

The most common bird on the beach is, of course, the Gull. There are many kinds of Gull, but they are all scavengers, usually eating dead things that wash up on the beach, stealing another bird's catch or young or hovering around shrimp trawlers. An interesting behavior of some Gulls is they will pick up an oyster from the shallows, fly high into the air and drop it onto the hard packed sand. This cracks open the oyster, and then the gull that dropped it is in competition with the others to get to it first. If you see a gull that makes you laugh, its a Laughing Gull, which makes a sound so like a human laugh its contagious. Other common Gulls here are the Herring Gull and the Ring-billed Gull. Herring Gulls are quite large - about 25" long. They have a yellow bill with a red dot at the tip . Ring-billed Gulls are about 19" long and a yellow bill with a black ring around it.

If you see a Gull-like bird that is actually working for its living by diving for food, its probably a Tern. There are many kinds of Tern, but common characteristics in this part of the country are white or light color with a black crown and a notched or forked tail.

A bird that looks somewhat like a Tern is a Black Skimmer. This bird flies just above the water and plows the surface of the water with its open beak, waiting to snap shut on any prey it contacts.

You might be looking out the window of your rental property some day and see what appears to be an island on the ocean that wasn't there earlier. Get out the binoculars and you will see it's thousands of birds floating together in the water. These are Scaup, a type of duck, and what you see is called a "raft" of Scaup.

If you are on the beach and see a large bird circling high overhead and looking like an Eagle, it's probably an Osprey. Like Eagles, Osprey were affected by DDT and almost became extinct. Even ten years ago an Osprey sighting on Hilton Head was rare. Fortunately the population has bounced back and sightings are now common. Keep an eye on this bird. When it sees a fish it will dive from great height at high speed and snatch up the fish with its razor sharp talons. It's quite a sight to see and sometimes happens close to the beach. You can see Osprey nests on TV antenna and other towers. Recently there have been sightings of bald Eagles on the Island. The local newspaper claims knowledge of three nesting pair in the general area. They, too are making a comeback.

Hilton Head's inland birds are much the same as those seen elsewhere. Songbirds include the Cardinal, Tufted Titmouse, Mocking Bird, Sparrow, Chickadee, Woodpecker and Wren. Grackles, a type of blackbird, are very common and very noisy. The males are an iridescent black and the females are brown. Ring-necked Turtle Doves are becoming increasingly common. They are a smoky beige in color, with a black band at the back of their necks. These birds can be seen pretty much throughout the year. Finches, Warblers, Hummingbirds, various Ducks, and Vireos, among others, are migratory visitors. This picture is of a Red Tail Hawk, common on Hilton Head. They are the squirrel's nemesis.

Bird watching

Other than the beach, the best places for bird watching on Hilton Head are the Sea Pines Forest Preserve and the Audubon Newhall preserve on Palmetto Bay road (off island is the Pinckney preserve, also popular among birders).

Reptiles

Alligators
Alligators are perhaps our best known wildlife. For the most part they live in the many lagoons

throughout Hilton Head. Alligators are cold-blooded (they have no mechanism to regulate body temperature) so they rely on their environment to survive. During cooler weather alligators will come out of their lagoons and lie on the banks in the sun to raise their body temperature. In warmer weather they stay in the water to stay relatively cool. This means the best times to see alligators are the spring and fall, but exceptions are common. If a lot of rain has lowered the water temperature in the lagoons, the alligators will come out to sun themselves. It also seems sometimes they come out of the water just because they feel like it, for example, on a cloudy day. In Winter (October to March) alligators become dormant and hide in mud dens, so are rarely seen.

Alligators in Hilton Head can grow to about 12 feet in length. Those larger than that are generally "removed" because they scare people. We locals have an arrangement with the alligators: we leave them alone and they leave us alone. You would be wise to honor that arrangement. Alligators are not normally aggressive toward humans but they are dangerous. An alligator can outrun a horse for a limited distance. Human adults are too big to be alligator prey, but small children and pets are vulnerable, and an angry alligator knows no fear and will go after anything that bothers it. Here are some rules to keep you out of harm's way:

A mother alligator protecting its nest is about the only circumstance an alligator will attack without provocation. This could occur in wooded or brushy areas near lagoons. Nesting is typically May through August, and the mother protects the hatchlings for one to three years.

Feeding alligators is illegal for a good reason. If an alligator sees humans as a source of food, it stands to reason it will approach humans. Alligators lack social skills - they won't ask nicely for a handout. To feed an alligator is to sign its death warrant, for it will become aggressive and will soon be "removed" (yes, killed).

Never, ever, let small children or pets play in lagoons or on the banks of lagoons. Alligators are so fast a pet can vanish before its owner can take a deep breath.

If you catch a fish in a lagoon and an alligator wants it, give it up. Reeling in the fish close to you is a very bad idea, as the alligator will see you as competition for food.

If someone tells you there are no alligators in a given lagoon all they have done is display their ignorance about alligators. Alligators move around and frequently relocate. A male can cover 1,000 acres in search of mates.

There have been very rare instances of alligators at the beach. Alligators can stand salt water but prefer fresh or brackish, so an alligator at the beach is out of its normal environment and probably lost. Just keep away from it - if possible report it.

It has been said that the way to tell the length of an alligator is to measure the distance between its eyes in inches, which will tell you its length in feet. This sounds like a very bad idea if the alligator is alive.

Lizards and Salamanders

You will see creatures we tend to call lizards climbing up stucco walls and wood fences or sunning on decks. They are absolutely harmless to man, in fact, they eat insects to our benefit.

Children like to try to catch them and often end up with a wriggling tail in their hands, for these creatures will sacrifice their tail as a defense against predators because they will grow another to replace it. A lizard that is usually green and has a red throat that it can blow up like a tiny balloon is an "Anole". The Anole can change color to brown, especially in cool weather. Females have a dorsal stripe on their back. A less common lizard you might see is the Skink. Skinks favor woodlands and gardens and are very shy. They are thicker in the body than other species.

Turtles

The most common turtles spotted sunning themselves on the banks of lagoons are Yellow Bellied Sliders. They have yellow bellies (Duh!) and show some yellow on their heads and legs .Others you may see are Diamond Back Terrapins. They too have some yellow on their shells but not on their heads or legs. They can live in salt or brackish water. If you should get close enough to one to count the rings on the "diamonds" on its shell, you will know its age in years. These turtles were once popular as food for humans. [Thanks, Jon]

The sea turtle you might see will likely be a Loggerhead. These turtles can grow to enormous size, up to four feet in length and weighing 400 pounds. If you see one in the water you will get just a glimpse, as it will dive as soon as it senses your presence. Loggerheads are protected by federal law as an endangered species. In the spring and early summer, females crawl awkwardly up the beach, often at night, and dig a hole in the sand near the high tide line. They will deposit about 100 eggs in this hole and cover it with sand, then return to the sea. About two months later, one night the eggs will hatch and the baby

Loggerheads will rush to the ocean. Only one Loggerhead egg in 10,000 will result in a hatchling becoming an adult. Their enemies are Raccoons and Ghost Crabs that eat the eggs, man, who sometimes regards the eggs as toys or in some cases a delicacy or aphrodisiac, fish and birds of prey that eat the hatchlings, and one unusual problem. Loggerhead hatchlings are guided to the ocean by the reflection of starlight on the water.

If people who occupy properties on or near the ocean have lights on at night during hatching season, the light and reflections produced confuses the hatchlings, who may head inland to certain death from dehydration or predation. Another Loggerhead killer is trash - balloons, plastic bags, Styrofoam™, etc. that they might mistake for food. The laws that protect Loggerheads provide extremely severe penalties for anyone who disturbs a nest or interferes with the hatchlings rush to the sea. You might be surprised to learn the law also requires lights visible from the beach to be extinguished or shielded from May 1 to October 31. The penalty for not doing so can be a fine of $895.00. If you should be fortunate enough to see a nest hatch, stay away from it, and do not illuminate a flashlight or cigarette lighter. Those who think they can circumvent those rules are often surprised by the volunteers who patrol the beaches at night to protect the nests and hatchlings. If you see a problem with Loggerhead nests or hatchlings, call the Coastal Discovery Museum at 843-689-6767 or the Sheriff at 843-785-3618. Do not try to help - fines go to six figures and jail time can be imposed.

Snakes

There are many species of snakes in South Carolina. I see a snake on Hilton Head on the average of once every two years, but I don't spend a lot of time in the woods. Most snakes are at least as afraid of humans as we are of them, and will try hard to avoid us. That said, I would encourage golfers looking for a wayward ball in the woods to make a lot of noise, sweeping the underbrush with their club. Poisonous snakes that could be found on the island are:

Coral snake. Usually small, burrows in the ground, very strong venom. Very rare in South Carolina. It is banded with red, black and yellow bands, but so are many other snakes. If the bands are yellow-red-yellow remember "kill a fellow".

Cottonmouth (AKA Water Moccasin) Is aquatic, may flee if approached or may display a huge white open mouth as a threat. They can get very large, up to several feet.

Rattle snake. I have heard of one being spotted on the island, when habitat was being disturbed during the construction of the Cross-island Expressway. They also can get very large.

Copperhead. Freeze at danger rather than run away, but not particularly aggressive. This is the only poisonous snake I have seen here (one sighting).

Hilton Head overall does not provide good habitat for snakes. It's too built out and there are too many people, so if you want to see snakes there are many better places.

You might see legless lizards that looks a lot like snakes except they have ear holes and moveable eyelids.

Frogs and Toads

If you have never felt a tree frog stick to your arm you have missed a neat feeling and an amazing natural phenomenon. These small, light green frogs appear to have suction cups on their toes, and can be seen sticking to sliding glass doors at night in the presence of outdoor lights that attract the insects they eat. But those are not suction cups! A suction cup that tiny could not have any effect on your skin - especially a hairy arm. As hard as it is to believe, those little round toes have on them tiny "hairs", thousands of them, so small they can actually grab individual molecules of whatever surface they cling to, including glass. What will mother nature think of next!. I am very fond of frogs.

It's a treat to take a walk at night after a rain and listen to the "peepers" and "croakers" at a pond or lagoon. When you try to get too close, suddenly the din turns to total silence. You probably know frogs and toads lay eggs which hatch tadpoles, who live in water and have gills. After a time they loose their tails and morph into their final form. I am always amazed that a dry area that turns into a pool of water after a heavy rain will suddenly be populated by hundreds of tadpoles overnight. Most of the time the pool will dry up before the tadpoles can become frogs, and they perish, but not always. Toads, unlike frogs, have a defense mechanism other than flight. Most toads have glands behind their eyes extending backward that secrete a milky substance that discourages their enemies, such as dogs.

Dolphins

Dolphins are mammals, not fish (there is a dolphin fish, known in restaurants as mahi-mahi).

David Mills

Technically, they are "toothed whales" , with only one blowhole (nostril). They breath air, are warm-blooded, bear live young, and suckletheir young. Mothers take care of their young during their first year. They can grow up to 12 feet in length and 800 Lbs. in weight and can swim at speeds up to 45 Mph. Since Dolphins are air breathing they are easily spotted when they surface for air. You will hear a telltale "whoosh" as the dolphin expels used air. They are adapted to breath infrequently by virtue of muscles that store oxygen and the ability to expel almost all the used air in their lungs when they exhale (we expel only 10%). Dolphins locate their food (mostly fish) by making a click-like sound and listening for an echo. This is similar to sonar used by submarines and is called echolocation. Blind people who navigate using a cane they tap employ the same principle. Scientists believe dolphins communicate with each other using squeaks and whistles and are trying to learn their language with little success.

Dolphins abound in the waters around Hilton Head. You can see them from the beach or from a boat. About 200 of our dolphin population are permanent, but many more are migratory. Many dolphins are friendly to humans and will come up to a boat out of curiosity. There are several ways you can see dolphins from a boat:

Kayaking puts you as close as you can get to wildlife, however it limits your range (it does take some effort), and may not provide a dolphin experience. May not be desirable for non swimmers or non athletically inclined.

Zodiac boats also put you right where the action is. They hold six people (a few are larger) plus the captain and can go almost anywhere. You are almost certain to see dolphin.

Larger boats such as Gypsy, Vagabond, Adventure and others provide a more stable platform with amenities such as a bathroom, soft drinks and snacks.

If you go on your own, look for a shrimp trawler anchored with its nets raised. Chances are they are clearing their nets or their shrimp catch of collateral catch, such as squid, small fish, etc. This attracts small fish, which in turn attract dolphins. You might well be treated to an unforgettable sight. Also, in Broad Creek, just as you come to the first docks on the left, may be a dolphin named Blackbeard (for a black spot on his "chin") who might choose to come visit. Bang on the side of your boat to call him - he might come close enough to touch.

When you go dolphin watching, consider the distance from the marina to the area you will be going. You don't want to spend all your time getting there and getting back.

Furry creatures

Deer are so plentiful on Hilton Head, especially in the Plantations, they are considered pests by some people. Deer are most active at dusk (when humans go inside for dinner). In Sea Pines Plantation you can't drive two miles at dusk without seeing deer, which should be warning enough to drive with caution. Although deer tend to panic and act irrationally when frightened, if you drive slowly they are easy to avoid. Deer travel in groups, so if you see one cross the street you can bet more will follow. Sometimes residents, who should know better, will walk their dog off the leash. A dog will usually chase a deer, and a deer being chased could run into you, your car, or even your sliding glass door.

Raccoons are also common on Hilton Head. They might be cute, but they can create a terrible mess by getting into your trash can, which they will surely do if they smell food (they seem to be able to smell through plastic bags). Outside trash should be in a container with a raccoon-proof lid locked down. They are very clever and can even remove a bungee cord from a trash can lid.

Although rabies has not been a problem on Hilton Head, these creatures can carry rabies. Wild animals (or feral animals such as cats) should not be approached or touched. Any animal acting out of the ordinary (a raccoon out in daylight) should be avoided and reported. Feral cats are common in marinas and stables - caution children to leave them alone. A scratch could mean a series of precautionary injections. Rabies is almost 100% fatal.

Crustaceans

Common crustaceans on Hilton Head are crabs and shrimp. The most common edible crab here is the Blue Crab, which is actually mostly green, except for the legs. Blue Crabs can be caught in tidal lagoons or in the ocean or sound. Female crabs have prominent red tips on their claws (the girls paint their fingernails), while males have little red. You can also tell one from the other by turning them upside down and observing their "apron". The male has an apron shaped like the Washington Monument, the female like the Capitol Dome.

Other crabs are:

Ghost crabs, which live in holes in the sand above the high tide line. They are white and their body is rectangular, about 2 inches in size. They look much bigger because they have very long legs. Ghost crabs are mostly nocturnal, but sometimes can be seen scurrying into their holes in the daytime (they are very shy).

Fiddler crabs are abundant in the mud flats at low tide, They are smaller than a dime and live in holes they dig in the mud. The males have a single pincer claw, which they wave constantly to attract females. When the tide comes in, Fiddler crabs go into their holes and plug the openings with a mud plug, thus staying relatively dry. These crabs are also spooky - to see them you must be still, or they will vanish into their holes.

Hermit crabs live in discarded shells . As they grow, they outgrow the current shell and move to a larger one. Hermit crabs are common on the beach. If you pick up an enclosed shell (like a snail shell) from the shallows, it probably is occupied by a Hermit crab. Look in the opening and you will barely see its hard legs covering the opening and providing protection.

Stone crabs are less common. They can grow up to five inches in width, and are reddish brown in color. They have two large, bulky claws, more like lobster claws. Stone crabs cannot be taken (a claw may be removed) and are mentioned here only because their claws are powerful enough to inflict appreciable damage to a human finger. They do not swim and are found on jetties.

Horseshoe crabs are misnamed - they are not crabs at all - they are related to spiders. Their large shells, up to 8 inches across, are common on the beaches, sometimes including legs and their spiny tail, . Horseshoe crabs are fierce looking but completely harmless to humans. They have been on this planet since before the dinosaurs. Their blood is used in biological research because it is very sensitive to bacteria and is used to detect impurities in drugs. Horseshoe crabs harvested for their blood are tapped and returned to the water none the worse for wear.

SHRIMP

The shrimp caught in the waters off Hilton Head are Brown shrimp, Pink shrimp and White shrimp. Everybody has an opinion as to which is better eating, but the fact is most shrimp consumed here are previously frozen farm-raised shrimp of foreign origin and are actually Pacific White shrimp. You can buy locally caught shrimp in stores, directly from the trawlers, or off the back of pickup trucks (off island). If you do, you should know the inedible head of a shrimp comprises about a third of its body weight - in other words, 3 pounds of shrimp with heads on is equivalent to two pounds with heads removed ($6 a pound with heads on = $9 with heads off).

Be knowledgeable when you shop for "fresh" shrimp - to me, previously frozen shrimp are not fresh because if you freeze them again they will have an unpleasant texture. South Carolina has three shrimping seasons, the start and end dates of which vary according to the condition of the shrimp population. The May - June season produces "white roe" shrimp; June - August is brown shrimp season; and August - December is for white shrimp. If the shrimp trawlers are not running (January to May), the "fresh" shrimp on pickup trucks and even at the docks are not fresh local shrimp by my definition.

Our local shrimp industry, like elsewhere in this country, is in sharp decline, with catch down by 2/3 from 2000 to 2005 because of environmental regulations, fuel prices, competition from foreign suppliers and a decline in the number of shrimp due to habitat damage. Grocery stores and some restaurants now advertise "wild American shrimp", which are chemical free. Expect to pay a premium for them - they are worth it. Foreign shrimp farms liberally use an antibiotic chloramphenicol, which is banned in the USA and is linked to human aplastic anemia and other health problems. *(Source: http://www.foodandwaterwatch.org/fish/shrimp/health-impacts)*

Flora

Some of our trees and other plants do not exist "up North", so they might be new to you. The huge, sprawling trees often draped in Spanish Moss are Live Oaks. They look nothing like northern Oaks until you see their acorns, which are the same. Live Oaks are evergreens, but they do change their leaves every year, The new leaves push off the old ones in March, giving the appearance of the trees being constantly in leaf.

The trees that look like palm trees are actually palmetto trees. Their seeds are berry-like, not coconuts or dates.

The pine trees you see here are mostly Loblolly Pines. The are the source of our garden mulch, Pine Straw, and in February and early March are the source of pine pollen, a yellow powder that covers everything and triggers allergic reactions. There are other types of pines, each of which grows in a different environment, such as the Pond Pine, which grows in areas that are wet much of the time. Pine trees have branches on just the top part of the trunk. The conifers you see with branches nearly to the ground are Red Cedar trees.

Spanish Moss is not moss at all, its an epiphyte, an air plant that derives all its needs from rainwater and sunlight. It does no harm to its host, as it is not parasitic. Some visitors collect Spanish Moss to use as mulch for potted houseplants. You need to know that it is often host to Chiggers, which are nasty little insects that bite humans and leave itchy red spots that are quite uncomfortable. Rumor has it you can put Spanish moss a Ziplock® bag as soon as you collect it, then put it in the microwave for a few seconds to kill the chiggers without harming the plant. We have not tried that because it seems like a good way to make a mess.

Plants to watch out for include poison ivy, often found growing up the trunks of trees, oleander, which is toxic if eaten, sand spurs, which are found on grassy fields by people walking barefoot (ouch!), and Yucca, a leafy plant with sharp spikes on the ends of the leaves that can deliver a painful puncture. Even pine cones need delicate handling, as some have sharp spikes.

The dunes you cross to get to the beach are home to several different plants, the most common of which is Sea Oats. They, along with other plants and grasses trap the sand as it is carried past by the wind, causing the dunes to slowly rise. The dunes are our only protection from storm surge caused by high tides and high winds. For that reason it is illegal to walk on the dunes, which are easily destroyed. Please be sure to use the manmade crossovers when going to or from the beach.

Free fun activities

Vacations can put a big dent in the family budget. There are many things to do on Hilton Head besides going to the beach that cost nothing. Here are some summer activities:

On Fridays, from 7 to 10 PM, Shelter Cove Town Center has a <u>sunset celebration</u>. The setting is informal, featuring live music, bounce houses and face painting for the kids, and occasionally some other entertainment. Bring a blanket or folding chairs and sit on the lawn.

On Thursdays, Shelter Cove Town Center shows <u>free movies</u>. Bring beach chairs or blankets and watch from the lawn. Starts at 9:00 PM.

Note: A free shuttle at Shelter Cove Town Center will bring you from the remote parking.

The action at Shelter Cove , on Tuesdays<u>, Summer Jams</u> starts with a community market and kids activities including a bungee jump, bounce houses, a rock wall, and a zip line. Then, From 7 to 9 PM are summer jams concerts lead up to a fireworks display at nightfall.

Also at Shelter Cove (by the Neptune statue), <u>Harbourfest</u> provides family entertainment with arts and crafts and fun for kids Monday through

Friday. There are two Shannon Tanner shows: 7:00 and 8:30 PM. Cappy the Clown will entertain there from 6 to 9 PM.

Shelter Cove also has Parrott Palooza Thursdays, when Shannon and the Oyster Reefers play a tribute to Jimmy Buffet at 7:00 PM

Coligny Plaza, at the beach, has entertainment every night, ranging from magic shows to live music to a dance party to team trivia night.. The fun starts at 6:30 and goes to 8:30 PM.

Harbour Town is the venue for the famous Gregg Russell performances which have enchanted kids for two generations. Kids vie to be picked to sing or perform and Gregg entertains with music from 8:00 to 9:30 PM every night except Saturday.

Lawton Stables has a free petting zoo, and horse lovers enjoy bringing treats of apples or carrots to the horses in the paddock any time.

The 605 acre Sea Pines Forest Preserve is a great place for a picnic or barbecue. You can also fish the lakes, take long walks and observe alligators and other wild life.

The Salty Dog has periodic events geared toward families and kids. There is live music every night featuring Dave Kemmerly, Bruce Crichton or Trevor Harden at the docks. In the Courtyard in front of Jake's Cargo enjoy Kids Fun from 6:30 to 8:15 PM. Saturday is juggling with Ben, Sunday and Tuesday is Carnival Night with Steve, Monday, Thursday and Friday the Music Lady entertains and on Wednesday DJ Anneliza hold a kids dance party. They also have a hula hoop contest and chalk art for kids

The Sea Pines Beach Club provides restrooms, outdoor showers and foot wash, and plenty of bike (but not car) parking. They often have live entertainment in the afternoons.

Pinckney Island National Wildlife Preserve is a great place to walk or bike and observe nature or for salt water fishing.

Audubon Newhall Preserve is a 50 acre nature preserve where you can hike and see a rare pocosin (bog). Sadly, it was badly damaged by hurricane Matthew.

The Island Winery offers free wine tasting from 12:30 to 5:30 PM Monday through Saturday.

The Island Distillery offers guided tours and tastings from March through September.

A complimentary golf clinic and exhibition is available on Mondays from 4:00 to 4:45 PM at the Palmetto Dunes Jones course.

SondorBlue, a group of young musicians, play a wide variety of music under the Liberty Oak in Harbour Town on Saturdays from 7:30 to 9:30 PM.

Christmas lights can be seen, typically between Thanksgiving and Christmas or a little later at : Shelter Cove Town Center, Shelter Cove Marina, Hilton Head Fire and Rescue #3 (534 Wm. Hilton Pkwy., next to the First Presbyterian Church and Bargain Box), South Beach Marina, Harbour Town marina, and Compass Rose Park.

Nature and Eco Tours

Enjoying nature on the water.
If you don't mind providing the locomotion, kayaking is an excellent way to see dolphins and shore birds. Tour guides are versed in the local wildlife and talk about the flora and fauna seen on the tour. They also know where to go to find dolphin. Seeing a dolphin from a kayak is quite a

thrill because you are so close, but it can be intimidating to some.

Zodiac boats are inflatable boats with rigid hulls. They hold up to six people plus the captain (a few might hold more if the captain is licensed for more). They are low in the water, so provide a good platform for observing dolphins up close. Going out on a zodiac, you will also have an expert guide and will be in a small group. Zodiacs have a greater range than kayaks, so they can go farther to find dolphins. Also, you don't have to paddle them. Here are some places that provide eco tours on zodiacs.

Commander Zodiac at the South Beach Marina in Sea Pines plantation. 843-671-3344. They use Zodiac boats (rigid bottom inflatable sides).

Island Explorer has both zodiac type boats and deck boats. They hold either six or twelve passengers. They operate from the docks at the Old Oyster Factory. 843-785-2100.

Other companies offer nature tours on small, six passenger boats.

If there are more than six people in your party and you want to be together, there are enviro tour boats that can hold more passengers but are still small enough to provide a close-up view. Besides Island Explorer, above, two of these are the SS Pelican (16 passengers) and the Island Queen, (40 passengers) which is wheelchair accessible . It operates out of Broad Creek Marina. 843-681-2522. The Dolphin Seafari atPalmetto Bay Water Sports holds 15 passengers. 843-785-2345. You can call the various marinas for information about others.

For those who like to sail, sail boats and sailing catamarans are available for eco tours also. For example: Cheers, a 47 foot sailing yacht, which sails out of Hudson's Restaurant landing. From my personal experience these are more to be enjoyed for sailing than for nature. Pau Hana and Flying Circus are sailing catamarans operating from the Palmetto Bay Marina 843-686-2582. Harbour Town Marina has H2O Let's Go Sailing, with two distinctly different boats 843-671-4386.

Some people prefer a stable viewing platform with amenities such as restrooms and snacks and beverages available. Some larger power boats that go out on dolphin watches are:

Gypsy, a 65 foot boat, which is docked at the South Beach Marina in Sea Pines Plantation. Gypsy offers not just dolphin watches but a "kids cruise" which adds cast netting for shrimp, pulling up crab traps that have previously been set, and shark fishing. 843-363-2900. Has a restroom.

Another eco cruise especially (but not exclusively) enjoyed by children is the Tammy Jane, a trawler where passengers learn all about shrimp trawling and are treated to a demonstration. You never know what will come up in the nets: squid, puffer fish, shrimp, crabs etc. Located at Skull Creek at Hudson's Seafood House. 843-384-7833.

The Holiday (80 feet) operates from Shelter Cove. 843-785-4558.

The Vagabond, (82 feet) in Harbour Town marina. 843-842-4155.

An interesting new excursion is aimed at nature photographers. Salt Marsh Photographic Cruises offers boat trips in the salt marsh guided by an experienced photographer. Departs from the Hilton Head Boathouse on Marshland Rd. 843-290-2720.

Live Oac is unique in that they operate at the North end of the island, near the bridge at the RV resort and marina

If you are experienced you can rent a boat or kayak and go out on your own. The best way to see dolphins, if you are fortunate enough, is to seek out a shrimp trawler that is at anchor with its nets up. Shortly after a trawler anchors, the crew usually clears the nets and the shrimp catch of collateral catch (small fish, squid, etc.) and dumps it overboard. This attracts small to medium fish, which in turn attract dolphin. If you are in a power boat and if the tide is running (either way) you should be able to nose into the current and apply just enough throttle to stay alongside the trawler for a long time. It's an experience you won't soon forget.

You will be almost certain to see several alligators on the H20 Alligator and Wildlife tour, a one-hour tour on an electric boat on a lake in the Sea Pines forest preserve. Be sure to bring your camera. 843-686-5323.

Enjoying nature on the beach.

The Coastal Discovery Museum offers a broad range of programs, including walking tours of the beach with a trained naturalist. In the loggerhead nesting season there is a chance of seeing a loggerhead nest and a slim chance of seeing hatchlings heading seaward at night. No matter what you want to do on Hilton Head, the Coastal Discovery Museum is well worth a visit. They are located at the Honey Horn Plantation at the Gum Tree road exit/entrance to the Cross Island toll road. 843-689-6767.

Enjoying nature on land.

To go bird watching and perhaps see alligators, turtles, deer and other critters, you might want to visit the Sea Pines Forest Preserve, a 650 acre forest with trails and lakes where you can go self-guided or with naturalist guides. For a guided tour, call Sea Pines Ecotours at 843-842-1979. Depending on the time of year you might be treated to a hayride (tractor drawn). You can also tour it on horseback by calling Lawton Stables at 843-671-2586. During egret nesting season, don't miss the Rookery, an island in the preserve where hundreds of egrets and herons nest.

Other popular places to go are the Audubon Newhall Nature Preserve off Palmetto Bay road between the foot of the cross-island bridge and Sea Pines circle, and the Pinckney Island Sanctuary. Both of these offer self-guided tours. The Coastal Discovery Museum offers guided nature walks on Pinckney island and sometimes at the Audubon

Preserve, programs are conducted by the Audubon Society. 843-785-5775.

The ideas presented above are a sample of what's available for visitors to enjoy. We make no representation regarding any of the companies or organizations listed, and they have not paid to be included.

Kayaking

In recent years, Americans have become increasingly health conscious and nature oriented. Kayaking is a great way to enjoy nature and get in some good exercise. No experience is needed - the kayak rental companies will teach you all you need to know. You need reasonable upper body strength and decent coordination - that's all. Life jackets are often required to be worn, (certainly non-swimmers must wear life jackets), and everyone should wear old clothes and foot covering that can get wet. There are kayak expeditions for dolphin and bird watching, for viewing the sunset, for full moon enjoyment and even for fireworks at Shelter Cove. Discount coupons are common in local publications.

Kayaks come in many varieties: one or two passenger, sit on or sit in, with or without a rudder.

If you have not been kayaking before (canoeing doesn't count) you should go on a tour. Otherwise you can rent a kayak and go off on your own. The tours generally offer instruction and guides who are knowledgeable about the area and its nature.

When planning your kayak trip, consider which goals you have in mind, then decide where you want to go. For example dolphin are best spotted in the Calibogue Sound (a few are in the lower reaches of Broad Creek). Birds are seen everywhere, but you are more likely to see some up close in the smaller waterways, such as Jarvis Creek (on the North End near Jenkins Island) or Calibogue Creek (near the mouth of Broad Creek) or Baynard Cove (near Braddock Cove in South Beach) ,as well as around the Pinckney Island Wildlife Refuge. The waters in the smaller waterways are smoother than in Broad Creek (some mild boat wakes) or in the Calibogue Sound, which can get quite choppy on windy days.

The tides are something to think about as well. At or near low tide some waterways are inaccessible, and if you depart from land, it might be quite muddy. At or near high tide is generally the best time to go. The tide can also affect the level of difficulty. Tidal currents can be quite swift and can catch you unprepared. I have seen a kayak swept from Braddock Cove to Harbourtown in a matter of minutes. Going against the tidal current can require considerable attention and athleticism. Conversely, the tide could make it easy if in your favor. Think about going when the tide is full in (slack tide), when there is little current. Inexperienced kayakers should not attempt to go to Daufuskie Island because the tidal currents can be very strong and boat wakes and wind driven chop (waves) can be brutal. If you go for the Shelter Cove fireworks, you should know in the summer dozens of power boats show up for the event, and you will be returning in the dark in a tiny kayak. Guided tours will manage to the tidal currents and might be a better solution for those without experience.

Listed here are some kayak rental and excursion companies in alphabetical order. We make no representation regarding these companies. This summarized information is provided to give you an idea who to call to get complete information.

<u>H2O Sports</u> Harbourtown. Guided tours or rentals.

<u>Hilton Head Outfitters</u> offers guided tours in the Palmetto Dunes lagoon system which has 12 miles of very calm waters. They have on-line reservations.

<u>Jarvis Creek Water Sports</u> Jarvis Creek behind the Crazy Crab North end provides another location with calm waters. Tours and rentals.

<u>Kayak Hilton Head</u> is located at Simmons Landing, next to the Broad Creek Marina. Tours and rentals.

<u>Outside Hilton Head</u> has two locations: Shelter Cove Marina and Hudson's Restaurant. They provide dolphin watches, kids' summer camp, fireworks, fishing, Pinckney Island Wildlife Refuge and Daufuskie Island. they have guided tours and kayak rentals.

<u>OneHHI</u> is in the Palmetto Bay Marina (pots Mattthew)

<u>Sea Monkeys</u> has kayak rentals and nature tours in Skull Creek at the north end. They are near the Pinckney Island nature preserve.

<u>Water Dog Outfitters</u> out of the Old Oyster Factory restaurant docks. Tours around Pinckney Island or on Broad Creek. Will rent to experienced kayakers.

Wave Runners

Wave runners are something like floating motorcycles. They are not the same as Jet Skis. You sit astride and steer with handle bars. They are propelled by an engine that inhales water and pumps it out a nozzle which swivels to provide steering. They can accommodate from one to three people, depending on the model. As a rule, three passenger wave runners are restricted to one adult and two children. Riders wear a wrist strap connected to a kill switch which shuts the engine off if the rider falls off (an infrequent event) so the machine stops. You will see a demonstration of how to get back on in the water. The rental companies operate on specific schedules, so you will need advance reservations. Generally a credit card is required for that, so be sure you ask about their policy regarding inclement weather.

Some companies require a driver's license and all have age restrictions for the driver. Children must be accompanied by an adult (they can steer if you let them). Wave runners are very fast and have no brakes, so careless operation can result in tragic consequences. Life jackets are a must. It is important to stay well away from other wave runners (they can turn on a dime) and boats. You are not supposed to jump boat wakes with a wave runner. In my opinion people with bad backs shouldn't go on wave runners (personal experience).

There are three locations on Hilton Head where rental wave runners can be operated: the Calibogue Sound, Broad Creek and Skull Creek. As can be expected, the waters of Broad Creek and Skull Creek are generally calmer than in the sound, though there may be some speed restricted "no wake" zones (not in the sound). Some people prefer a bumpy ride and some don't.

Here are <u>some</u> companies that rent wave runners, in alphabetical order. We make no representation regarding these companies.

If your company is not listed here and you want it to be, use the "Your Comments, Please" form. There is no cost to you.

<u>H2O Sports</u> operates out of the Harbour Town marina and in the Calibogue sound, rents singles for $109/Hr, doubles for $119/Hr. One person must be 18 years or older with photo ID. 843-363-2628.

<u>Island Water Sports</u> at the south Beach Marina in Sea Pines rents wave runners in the Calibogue sound for $109 for 75 minutes single, $119 double.

<u>Sea Monkeys</u> is located at the north end and offers wave runner rentals in Skull Creek, in the Pinckney Island vicinity, which is typically less crowded than south end venues. Will rent to 16 year olds with valid driver's license. $100 single, $110 double $115 triple for 75 minutes. 843-842-4754.

Resorts and Plantations

Hilton Head Island is a beautiful place, but navigating it can be confusing. While many areas are free and open to the public, they can still be hard to find because of how the Island is set up. Much of Hilton Head is segmented into gated communities, also known as plantations. While some of them are private residential communities for people who live on the island year-round, there are others with resorts, golf courses, businesses and places to visit that are open to visitors. Here is a quick run down of the different gated communities that make up Hilton Head Island and what you'll find inside.

Windmill Harbour
161 Harbour Psge. | Private
One of the smaller private gated communities on the island, Windmill Harbour is the first visitors pass when they come onto the island. Meant for year-round residents, Windmill Harbour offers many amenities, mainly focusing on yachting and boating.

The marshlands surrounding Pinckney Island and the open water access from Skull Creek, Calibogue Sound and the Atlantic Ocean provide the perfect views and water access to Windmill Harbour. The homes are filled with beautiful pastel colors, and while it is one of the smaller gated communities on the Island, 80% of the houses have views overlooking the water. The perks of living here or renting a home in Windmill Harbour is all about the boating, which is why it is home to the South Carolina Yacht Club.

For more information, call Windmill Harbour at (843) 681-9235 or go to windmillharbourmarina.org.

Spanish Wells
65 Headlands Dr. | Semi-Private
While secluded, Spanish Wells is more than worth the visit. The second smallest community, with 350 acres and only about 200 homeowners, Spanish

Wells provides a private secluded place away from all the hubbub that the very center of the Island brings and does not offer vacation rentals or packages for visitors. Being two miles from the Cross Island Bridge, and three miles from the north end, Spanish Wells, while being right on the water, has a central location making it easy to access pretty much anything on the Island in mere minutes.

They house two miles of walking and jogging trails as well as Hilton Head's only waterfront clubhouse complete with a swimming pool and cabana, and a new pro shop and grille. Four Har-Tru tennis courts are lit for night play as well as safety along the nine-hole Cobb golf course with a full practice facility.

For more information, call Spanish Wells Plantation at (843) 341-3188 or go to spanishwellsplantation.com.

Hilton Head Plantation
7 Surrey Ln. | Private
After passing Windmill Harbour along William Hilton Parkway, Hilton Head plantation is located a little further down the road, home to four golf clubs and 10,000 year-round permanent residents. Homes are privately owned within the plantation, but if visitors are headed to the golf courses and clubs they are allowed within the security gates. With three parks, an Olympic-size swimming pool, two conservancies for nature preservations and 12 Har-Tru tennis courts, it is one of the biggest and most popular private gated communities for permanent residents on the Island.

Four golf clubs are located inside of Hilton Head Plantation, and if you are a member or visiting a member of any of the clubs, you are allowed access through the 24/7 security gates surrounding the community. Two of the golf clubs, the Oyster Reef Golf club and the Country Club of Hilton Head, are both semi-private clubs. The other two, Bear Creek Golf Club and Dolphin Head Golf Club, are both privately owned and operated within Hilton Head Plantation.

For more information, call Hilton Head Plantation at (843) 681-8800 or go to hiltonheadplantation.com.

Indigo Run
103 Indigo Run Dr. | Private
Right across the street from Hilton Head Plantation is Indigo Run, just past Main Street Village, the local Wal-Mart, Barnes and Noble and Publix. It is located more so out of the thick of the tourist areas, and on the residential side at the north end of the Island. Visitors can rent homes and villas on

a nightly or weekly basis, but this community has much more full time residents than vacationers.

Home to the Golden Bear Golf Club and The Golf Club, Indigo Run is perfect for residential families on the Island. It is close enough to many necessities while still having privacy away from many of the crowds that swarm the Island during the spring and summer seasons.

For more information, call Indigo Run (843) 681-9195 or go to indigoruncoa.org.

Palmetto Hall
108 Fort Howell Dr. | Private
Sandwiched between Hilton Head Plantation and Port Royal Plantation Beach House, Palmetto Hall Plantation is one of the smaller, more elite sections of private housing on the Island. Filled with beautiful grandiose homes and 36 holes of scenic golf, Palmetto Hall Plantation caters to

those wishing to stay within a private gated community year-round.

Palmetto Hall does offer wedding packages for their beautiful scenery and Heritage golf packages for those golfers coming to the island to play or watch the RBC Heritage Golf Tournament held every April.

For more information, call Palmetto Hall at (843) 342-2582 or go to palmettohallgolf.com.

Port Royal
45 S Port Royal Dr.| Semi-Private
Port Royal Plantation is located in what is called the "heel" of the Island. The entrance into the private plantation is right at the curve in the road on William Hilton Parkway. Most of the homes are privately owned and lived in year round, but some are rented out individually during the busy summer season.

Visitors will find the Westin Hilton Head Resort and Spa, as well as three golf courses, four tennis courts and an Olympic-size swimming pool, Port Royal Plantation offers great amenities for permanent residents and the vacationers.

Port Royal is home to 886 single-family homes with more space to grow. There are 84 undeveloped plots for those who wish to build their perfect house on a southern tropical island. For the history buffs, Port Royal is home to two historical sites from the civil war and is also home to the Spanish-American War Steam Gun. For more information, call Port Royal Plantation at (843) 681-5114 ext. 104 or go to portroyalplantation.net.

Palmetto Dunes
4 Queens Folly Rd. | Semi-private mostly Public
Sitting mid-island, Palmetto Dunes Oceanfront Resort is one of the most well-known vacation areas on the Island next to Sea Pines Resort. Home

to both the Hilton Head Marriott Resort and Spa and the Omni Hilton Head Oceanfront Resort, Palmetto Dunes also owns and operates the Shelter Cove Harbour and Marina, next to the new Shelter Cove Towne Centre.

Filled with tons of activities from shopping to yachting, Shelter Cove Harbour provides everything the Palmetto Dunes guests could want, including the fact that it is across the street from the resort itself. This gives renters, vacationers and homeowners a sense of privacy but also unparalleled access to some of the best activities, shops and restaurants on the Island.

Within the resort itself there are 11 miles of lagoons for kayaking or canoeing as well as nature trails, over 25 tennis courts, three golf courses and a private residential community within the resort called Leamington.

For more information, call Palmetto Dunes Oceanfront Resort at (888) 322-9091 or go to palmettodunes.com.

Yacht Cove
Yacht Cove Dr. | Private
Hidden between the Long Cove Club and Shelter Cove sits Yacht Cove, the smallest private gated community on the Island. With only 74 single family homes, 47 townhouses and 54 villas, Yacht Cove is a close-knit community of islanders who live here year round. Vacation rentals are not available.

Affordable options and a small community make this area perfect for families with small children. Volunteers are welcome to help out to maintain the grounds, and keep H.O.A. costs low, which many of the other communities on the Island do not offer. Living here is all about helping your neighbor, and helping yourself.

For more information, call Jaque Qualls, director of the Yacht Cove Hotline, at (843) 785-8380 or go to yachtcovehhi.com.

Long Cove Club
44 Long Cove Dr. | Private
Down the street from Palmetto Dunes is one of Hilton Head's best kept secrets: Long Cove Club. Another small private residential community on the Island, Long Cove Club on Hilton Head is also one of the most private and secure. Meant for year-round and permanent living, Long Cove Club was built in the early 1980s and is considered one of the Island's most private areas. Located just south of mid-island, the Long Cove Club has access to everything around it, including deep water access through their private Broad Creek harbour and marina, without having to stray far from home.

Golf Digest has rated the Long Cove Club's course #1 in South Carolina for 10 consecutive years and since the opening of their tennis facility in 2002, it has since become a world-class tennis destination for pros and amateurs alike.

For more information, call Long Cove Club at (800) 995-4069 or go to longcoveclub.org.

Wexford
1000 William Hilton Parkway, Suite J-18 | Private
Right next to Long Cove Club sits Wexford Plantation, a private residential community. Known for their signature Arnold Palmer Golf course, Wexford provides a quiet and serene place for their residents smack in the middle of the Island, located within walking distance of fun filled activities.

Wexford has six tennis courts, a clubhouse, swimming pool, shared patio area for parties that all residents are welcome to use, and it is home to both the Family Circle Mixed Double tennis qualifier as well as the local USTA junior tennis tournament.

Hilton Head is all about sea life, and so Wexford Plantation is home to one of only three harbours along the eastern seaboard with a locking system and a 24/7 crew to maintain and open the gates for any of the residents.

For more information, call the Wexford Plantation (843) 686-6950 or go to wexfordplantation.com.

Shipyard
10 Shipyard Dr. | Semi-private
Located at the south end of the Island right before Sea Pines is Shipyard Plantation. A diverse place for residents, visitors and golfers to enjoy all the amenities the plantation has to offer. Golf courses, tennis courts, hiking, jogging and biking trails, a health spa and a great clubhouse for all residents

and visitors are just a few of the things Shipyard provides for their guests and permanent residents.

Their "mix and match" style golf, split between three courses and 27 holes of beautifully manicured greenery, is what sets Shipyard apart from the other golfing communities on the Island. The Brigantine, Clipper and Galleon courses all offer different and challenging shots for golfers.

Shipyard houses one of the biggest resorts on the Island, the Sonesta Resort. They offer room rentals, villas, suites of any size to help fit any and all vacation rental needs.

For more information, call Shipyard Plantation at (843) 785-3310 or go to shipyardhhi.com.

Sea Pines
32 Greenwood Dr. | Semi-private
The biggest plantation on Hilton Head, Sea Pines, takes up nearly a third of the Island. While it is the

biggest, it is also known as the first private plantation on the Island as well. Charles E. Fraser began building Sea Pines Plantation in 1956 to give native islanders a place to stay, and for those who wished to come and visit the Island, a great and safe place to do so.

Anyone who is not staying within the resort must pay a $6 entrance fee per person. Any bikes attached to the cars are charged an additional $1 per bike.

Sea Pines is home to Harbour Town, South Beach and Lawton Stables. With over five miles of shoreline, 100 tennis courts and a 605-acre forest preserve, Sea Pines has everything anyone could ever need while on vacation. The entire vacation could be spent within Sea Pines without having to leave, but who wouldn't want to see the rest of a tropical island?

Harbour Town is one of the landmark places on the Island, known for its red-and-white-striped lighthouse, restaurants and beautiful views of Calibogue Sound. It's at the Harbour Town Golf Links that PGA tour's RBC Heritage Golf Tournament is held every year. Thousands of people flock to Hilton Head to watch the tournament and bring in over $1.5 million into the economy each year. Sea Pines is a huge reason why Hilton Head is known as a premier golfing destination worldwide

Historic Sites on Hilton Head

Before Hilton Head Island became known as a place of luxurious hotels, perfect golf courses, lush gardens and hundreds of shops and restaurants; it was an island with a rich history and culture. Seek out and explore that culture next time you come to visit.

Coastal Discovery Museum

A great first stop in exploring Hilton Head Island's rich history is the Coastal Discovery Museum. The museum, housed in a former plantation house, is located on 68 beautifully preserved acres of forest, field and marsh. The museum offers permanent and rotating exhibits on the natural and cultural history of the island, from Native Americans before the settlement of Europeans, through the resort boom of the 1960s and 1970s. But perhaps even more impressive than the exhibits are the classes and tours the museum offers. You can learn how to weave traditional sweetgrass baskets perfected by the Gullah people of the island, or how to cast a net in the traditional Gullah style of fishing practiced here. You also can tour historic forts and learn the history of the Revolutionary War on the island. Set aside some time to explore not just the museum but to take advantage of the incredible programming.

Zion Chapel of Ease and Cemetery

All that is left of the chapel, once part of the Episcopal Church, is its still and haunting graveyard. In that graveyard, you'll find the Baynard Mausoleum, the oldest structure on the island.

Gullah Heritage Trail Tours

Take a tour and you'll learn more about the Gullah culture of the Sea Islands, including Hilton Head. The Gullah people are descended from enslaved West Africans who cultivated and harvested the famed Sea Islands Cotton. Because the Sea Islands were so isolated both before the Civil War and for the 100 years after freedom, accessible only by boat, the descendants of the enslaved people developed their own rich culture that preserves much of their African heritage; including literature and folklore, cuisine and dialect. Before the 1960s, the vast majority of people who lived in Hilton Head Island were descendants of slaves. The Gullah Heritage Trail Tours, led by people of Gullah descent who were born and reared on the island, include some of the most important sites on the island; giving visitors a sense of Gullah life on the island before the bridges and resorts massively changed both the landscape and the lifestyle.

Dye's Gullah Fixin's

Interested in experiencing more Gullah heritage? Food is an intrinsic (and delicious) part of any society, including Gullah culture. Head over to Dye's Gullah Fixin'srestaurant to experience some of the most authentic traditional Lowcountry cuisine, both in terms of ingredients and technique, that you'll find on Hilton Head. Because Dye cooks each dish to order, reservations are a must for dinner: Dye908@gmail.com or (843) 681-8106.r

Forts

Before its beaches were speckled with resorts and vacation homes, Hilton Head Island was speckled with forts. Its location and size made it strategically important for defending the South Carolina mainland. The Sea Islands make a chain across the coast. Control the narrow waterways between the islands, and you control who gets in and out by sea. Four forts were built on Hilton Head during the Civil War. The remains of Fort Mitchel, a Civil War fort made of earthen embankments (and only rediscovered when a local restaurant was being built) and Fort Howell, another Civil War earthen fort, will fascinate Civil War buffs. Fort Walker, best seen with a tour from the Coastal Discovery Museum, was one of the targets of the largest naval battle ever in U.S. waters, the Battle of Port Royal.

Mitchelville

When Union forces took Hilton Head on November 7, 1861, in the Battle of Port Royal, more than 1,000 Hilton Head Islanders became some of the first freed slaves of the Civil War. They founded the town of Mitchelville, the first freedmen's town in America. You can visit Mitchelville on one of the Gullah history tours on the island or take a drive down Beach City Road, past the churches, homes and school building still standing there today. Stop at Mitchelville Freedom Park on your way for the natural beauty, view of the site of the Battle of Port Royal and historical markers explaining much of the history of the area.

Harbor Town Lighthouse and Museum

The iconic lighthouse in Harbour Town was actually not built as a lighthouse at all. It was built as a tourist attraction when Hilton Head was first developed as a resort destination. But that in and of itself is an important part of the history of Hilton Head Island. Along with a beautiful view from the top, you'll have the chance to see historic photos and read the fascinating history of the island on placards lining the stairs to the top.

Accommodations

Types of Rental Accommodations on Hilton Head

Hilton Head offers a wide range of lodging properties in a wide range of prices. There are three basic types of lodging available:

Home and Villa Rentals

Homes and villas are generally rented through one of the many rental agencies on the island. They are economical for stays of more than a couple of days, especially for a family group, because they provide such amenities as a kitchen and living room and can include multiple bedrooms and bathrooms and often multiple television sets.

Pricing is a function of proximity to the beach, the number of bedrooms, the availability of a swimming pool, the quality of construction, and the season of the year. On a per bedroom basis they are usually more economical than comparable hotel rooms. There are four seasons for the purpose of pricing, but not all providers use the same dates. As always, you get what you pay for. For examples of pricing, click on "Find Accommodations", below.

Such accommodations vary from small, compact beach villas with mini kitchens to what would be considered full size apartments suitable for year around living to palatial homes worth millions. The terms "villa" and "condo" are often used interchangeably on Hilton Head. Either could describe a unit in a high rise building or an apartment or townhouse within a complex. They could describe a flat or a two or more story unit. Access for handicapped varies - some properties were built before laws mandating such access.

Amenities vary. Most properties have a swimming pool or access to one. Usually linens and towels are provided (often excluding beach towels). Typically the property is cleaned before guest arrival but not during the stay. Ask about access to clothes washers and dryers to ensure a supply of clean towels. Cookware, glasses, plates and flatware are almost always provided. If a microwave, multiple TVs, a DVD player, or Internet access are important to you ask about them. Also ask what size beds are in each room.

When you communicate with a rental agent, be sure to understand their terminology regarding proximity to the beach. Terms such as " ocean front" ,"ocean view",' "ocean side", " short walk to the beach" are not used consistently from one agency to the next. Be very specific about the distance to the beach and the view of the beach to avoid disappointment later. Also, for villas, ask about the size in square feet. A full size two bedroom villa should be over 1000 square feet and should have its own clothes washer and dryer within the unit.

The rental agent typically does not own the properties that are for rent; they are owned by individuals or companies and are furnished and decorated by their owners. Consequently the decor and condition of the properties varies widely, as do individual tastes. If you don't care much about those things, tell the agent and ask for a low rate for a tired property. If you are traveling with a client you want to impress, say so and perhaps go for a pricey VIP property. Male golf groups should be sure to specify they want a separate bed for each person.

The minimum age for those renting is governed by law and by the policy of the rental agent. Many agencies will not accept "spring breakers" because of bad experiences. If you are under 25 years old, make sure you say so to avoid being turned away when you arrive.

There are very few of these accommodations that permit pets. Most condo associations have banned pets even for the owners. Do not try to sneak a pet in - you will surely be found out and your vacation may be ruined. There are places on the island that board pets. When I travel I take mine to the Evergreen Pet Lodge. You can visit your pet there and if you are willing to pay extra they will walk dogs and provide other special treatment.

Hotels Motels and Inns

Rooms and suites are available all over Hilton Head island and range widely in price. They are your best bet for a stay of two days or less, and should be considered for a couple traveling alone and not needing a kitchen or extra space (some have kitchenettes). Accommodations range from luxury ocean front hotels to economical motels far from the beach. You can expect to have your room cleaned and fresh towels supplied daily. Very few permit pets.

Timeshares

Timeshares are condominiums that are sold by the week. In other words, one can buy week 27 (early July) at a given property and is then entitled to stay there every year at that particular time. If the owner of a particular week chooses not to use it, the management might rent it out. As a practical matter, most timeshare owners belong to organizations that exchange timeshares. If an owner chooses not to use a week, they will probably turn it over to the exchange organization to use in exchange for another location or week. As a result, timeshares are not widely available on the rental market. Some timeshare companies will offer a teaser rental rate to those willing to listen to a sales pitch which can be an hour or more in length and can be hard to resist. Other inducements to listen to a sales pitch include coupons for free golf or restaurant meals.

The End

CPSIA information can be obtained
at www.ICGtesting.com
Printed in the USA
LVHW102058120622
721098LV00004B/541